FROM DECISIONS TO DISCIPLES

FROM DECISIONS TO DISCIPLES

"Obeying the Divine Demand"

DR. RAY CUMMINGS

From Ray

To Jesus, my Lord and Savior . . . Thank You for commanding us to make disciples. Thank You for being a personal God who walks with Your children daily. Thank You for Your salvation and strength. Thank You for Your purpose over our lives and your power to make it happen!

To Amanda... Thank you for being the best example in my life of His love. I am so thankful for you and privileged to grow in Christ alongside you. You have been my greatest example of a true disciple of Jesus. I love you and I am overjoyed to walk this journey with you.

To Carter, Camron, Moses, and Mercy . . . Thank you for being you! I love the way God created each of you and am extremely proud of how God's hand is on each of your lives. You have given me so much joy and I am so thankful to be your father.

To those who read this book . . . Thank you for your desire to become His disciple and your willingness to obey His command to make disciples. May you one day hear Him say, "Well done!"

FROM DECISIONS TO DISCIPLES

"Obeying the Divine Demand"

Matthew 28:18-20 (NIV)

18 Then Jesus came to them and said,
"All authority in heaven and on earth has been given to Me.
19 Therefore go and make disciples of all nations,
baptizing them in the name of the Father
and of the Son and of the Holy Spirit,
20 and teaching them to obey everything I have commanded you.
And surely I am with you always, to the very end of the age."

Table of Contents

Foreword

The first thirty years of my ministry, I pastored churches in Mississippi, Kentucky, South Carolina, and Alabama. I had a deep commitment to evangelism and, while there was not much written then on discipleship, I was committed to assimilation. That meant I was constantly trying to get new believers connected to, and involved in, the local church. I adopted a philosophy that said, "**Evangelism without discipleship is exploitation of people.**" I wanted no part of any evangelism event without clearly knowing how follow up and discipleship was going to take place.

I moved from the pastorate to Director of Evangelism for the Alabama Baptist State Convention and served in the evangelism office for 27 years. I saw my commitment to evangelism and discipleship fleshed out all over the State of Alabama with its 3200 plus Baptist churches. That was emphasized in event evangelism, mass evangelism, as well as personal evangelism and church evangelism. I believed then, and now, that evangelism and discipleship are two wings on the same airplane. And just as no one would take off in an airplane with one wing, neither should anyone take off with a one wing approach to reaching people. Discipleship should go further than assimilation. Discipleship should take the new believer not to just Church involvement, but rather to a growing walk with Jesus until they are a disciple maker themselves.

This book by Dr. Ray Cummings will do just that. These thirteen chapters will take you from the "Five-Fold Commission of Christ" to "The Daily Development of Discipleship," all the way to a personal devotional study around the acrostic "B.I.B.L.E." I have known Ray Cummings for many years: preached for him, led in a revival in his church, and know his commitment to disciple making is a genuine call on his life and ministry. I pray as you read *From Decisions to Disciples*" you will make that same deep commitment in your life and ministry.

Dr. Sammy Gilbreath

Served as Director of Evangelism for the Alabama Baptist State Board of Missions for 27 years.

Chapter 1

The Five-Fold Commission of Christ

Welcome to the journey of discipleship. I must begin by confessing to you that, as a minister of over thirty years, I have not been discipled or discipled people as I should. For much of my adult life, I have been heavily involved with Bible study either through teaching or participating. However, recently the Lord has stirred my heart to what has been His command all along. God unmistakably revealed to me that His command in Matthew 28:18-20 was not to teach or participate in Bible studies, but to make disciples. This book is a collection of what God has taught me concerning discipleship over the last few years of my life. I have recently had the privilege of taking small groups of people through the process of biblical discipleship and the impact has been incredible. I am praying for you as you take this journey. I hope as God reveals Himself to you, that you will respond and see His purpose and power displayed through your life.

Jesus gave a clear command in His final commission to His first disciples. He did not stutter or make a suggestion. He stated a divine demand: "Make Disciples." Many churches today focus on getting people to make decisions. However, very few of those churches have a plan or process to make disciples.

Most of our present-day churches have a weekly worship service and Bible study hour. I must add here that if your church has an hour on the schedule entitled "Discipleship," that does not mean that biblical discipleship is taking place. Most of the time, that is just a label for another Bible study hour that occurs during the week. I do believe that studying God's Word is part of the process that leads to discipleship. Yet, just sitting in a class for an hour and listening to someone teach Scripture doesn't make you a disciple. Still very few local churches even schedule a third time for discipleship. What we won't even put third in importance, Jesus gave as His marching orders. What we don't even suggest, Jesus said, start with. What we push aside as optional, Jesus stated as paramount to be obeyed. When Jesus returns, His first words to His church just might be, "What are you doing?" or "Why aren't you doing what I demanded?"

Some call it His command. Others call it His commission. Still some call it His mandate. And everyone calls it "Great." But very few of those who call themselves "Christ-followers" follow His command to "make disciples." In fact, Jesus gave a five-fold commission to His church. There is one commission from Christ given in each of the Gospels and one stated in the book of Acts. Let's look at each one to get the big picture of what God's purpose is for His people.

Matthew 28:18-20

[18] *Then Jesus came to them and said, "All authority in heaven and on earth has been given to Me.* [19] *Therefore go and make disciples of all nations, baptizing them in the name of the Father and of the Son and of the Holy Spirit,* [20] *and teaching them to obey everything I have commanded you. And surely I am with you always, to the very end of the age."*

Matthew's commission gives us the **promise**. We will look at these three verses in detail in the next chapter. But God promises His power and presence as we go and make disciples.

Mark 16:15

15 He said to them, "Go into all the world and preach the gospel to all creation."

Mark's account states the **parameters**. Disciples of Christ are to "go into all the world" and proclaim the message "to all creation." We find the word "all" five times in these first two commissions. God has clearly called all of His converts to go to all of His creation.

Luke 24:46-49

[46] He told them, "This is what is written: The Messiah will suffer and rise from the dead on the third day, [47] and repentance for the forgiveness of sins will be preached in His name to all nations, beginning at Jerusalem. [48] You are witnesses of these things. [49] I am going to send you what My Father has promised; but stay in the city until you have been clothed with power from on high."

Our commission from Luke the physician centers on **preaching**. Verse 47 says that repentance and forgiveness will be preached to all nations. The message we should declare is in verse 46: "Jesus died and rose again on the third day!" We should continue His message preaching repentance and calling people to seek His forgiveness.

John 20:21

[21] Again Jesus said, "Peace be with you! As the Father has sent Me, I am sending you."

John's record of a commission from the Lord includes the **pattern**. The same way God sent Jesus; Jesus sends His disciples. Jesus came not to be served, but to serve and give His life as a ransom for many. (See Matthew 20:28 and Mark 10:45.) Jesus came to seek and save the lost. (See Luke 19:10.) Jesus came to give life more abundantly. (See John 10:10.) The purpose Jesus lived for is now the purpose His disciples live out.

Acts 1:8

8 But you will receive power when the Holy Spirit comes on you; and you will be My witnesses in Jerusalem, and in all Judea and Samaria, and to the ends of the earth."

The commission in Acts displays the promise of His **power**. No one has the power to become a disciple or to make one. Therefore, God sent His Holy Spirit to empower and enable His children to obey His commandments.

Thus, in His five-fold commission to His church; Jesus said the promise, specified the parameters, stated the preaching, set the pattern, and sent His power. Yet, isn't it interesting that of all five of these commissions, we only call one of them "The Great Commission?" The one distinction of the one we call "Great" is the only one that demands we "make disciples." You see, the problem is not that the world doesn't have enough Christians; it is that Christ does not have enough disciples.

It is time for the church to obey the divine demand. It is time to move people from decisions to discipleship. His church has His command. Let's go and make disciples!

Chapter 2

The Divine Demand from the Great Commission

Since Matthew 28:18-20 is "The Great Commission," we would do well to know the meaning of this message inside and out. This divine demand deserves a deeper study. In this chapter, we will look in detail at this command. Let's start in verse 18.

Matthew 28:18

18 Then Jesus came to them and said, "All authority in heaven and on earth has been given to Me . . ."

Who is the audience for this commission? Who is the "them" that Jesus came to? Matthew 28:16 informs us that the eleven disciples are the original hearers of the Great Commission and Jesus had appointed them to this meeting.

Matthew 28:16-17

16 Then the eleven disciples went away into Galilee, into a mountain where Jesus had appointed them. 17 And when they saw Him, they worshipped Him: but some doubted.

Some scholars believe that the 500 witnesses to the resurrected Christ mentioned in 1 Corinthians 15:6 were also there. But make no mistake, the first disciples of Jesus Christ are the distinguished guests of this mountain meeting. The command to make disciples was given to the first group that Jesus discipled. Jesus had modeled discipleship to them. Now they are to go make disciples of others. That commission has been handed down to all followers of Jesus Christ.

Matthew 28:17 ends with a startling statement, "but some doubted." This is at least the fourth resurrection appearance of Jesus to His disciples. Yet some still doubted. Did they still doubt that He was risen and alive? Or did they doubt their own ability to carry on as His disciples? If indeed it was the latter, Jesus will give them some incredible confidence and enough encouragement with how He both begins and ends His Great Commission.

Matthew 28:18 records Jesus' first words of this commission. Christ said, "All authority in heaven and on earth has been given to Me." There are two main Greek words in the New Testament for "power" or "authority." One of those words is *"dunamis."* This is where we get our English word dynamite. This word means "power, might, and force." However, that is not the word found in Matthew 28:18. The word for authority in this text is extremely interesting. It is the Greek word *"exousia."* This is a term that means "the power of influence. The ability or strength with which someone is endued." It actually comes from two Greek words: *"ek"* meaning "out from" and a form of the verb *"eime,"* which is the action word "to be." *"Eime"* is the main verb for the I AM statements of Jesus found in John's Gospel. If you take these two words together, *"exousia"* is defined as "Out of who I am." God has all authority in Heaven and on earth because of who He is. Out of all that

Jesus is, He gives the divine demand to His disciples. What an introduction!

Jesus also ends the Great Commission with an I AM statement.

Matthew 28:20

20 . . . And surely I am with you always, to the very end of the age."

Now, you can't see it in the English, but in the Greek the word "I" is written twice. In the study of Greek grammar, it is called the *ego eimi* construction. It is an emphatic construction. The *ego eimi* construction is the identical structure used in the seven I AM statements of Christ. *Ego* is the pronoun "I." *Eimi* is the main verb of this verse. This verb is in the following tense – present active indicative, first person singular. By itself, the verb translates as "I am." Together the *ego eimi* construction literally means, "I, I am." Most Greek scholars define it as, "I even I." Bible translators don't add the I twice, they just intensified the one "I" and said "Surely I" or "Lo I."

I find it extremely interesting that a form of the I AM statement bookends the Great Commission. Jesus says, "Out of who I AM, go and make disciples." Then after He gives the commission, Jesus says, "I even I will be with you always." If that doesn't give you confidence as you live out the Great Commission, I don't know what will! God gives you the command out of all that He is and Jesus Himself will be with you as you carry that command out. If you obey His command, you cannot fail! His command comes with His power and His presence!!

What is the command of the commission? Let's look between the I AM statements.

Matthew 28:19-20a

19 Therefore go and make disciples of all nations, baptizing them in the name of the Father and of the Son and of the Holy Spirit, 20 and teaching them to obey everything I have commanded you.

There are four commands found here in this middle section of Scripture. Only one of them is the divine demand. We will discuss them in order.

The first command is "Go." This word is in the following tense: aorist passive participle. It is also plural. So, all disciples are to go. Participle gives us the "ing" form of going. Passive means that the subject receives the action of the verb. Aorist means a once-and-for-all completed action that carries implications into the present and future. The best way to translate this first verb is "having gone." God already expects His followers to be in motion to make disciples. This can also mean that everywhere you go creates an opportunity for you to make disciples.

The second of these four verbs is the main imperative of the Great Commission. It is the verb *"matheteusate"* and means "make disciples." Now the word "make" is not in the original language. Translators add it to help the sentence flow better. It is simply the verb form of "disciple." Jesus is saying to His first disciples, "Go and disciple!"

"Make disciples here occurs in the aorist active imperative, second person plural tense. Active means do it right now! Imperative means it is not an option for the believer. It is a demand and a command. Plural again means for all Christ-followers. And aorist means it was a once-and-for-all command and God still expects it today and in the future!

This verb is where we get the word "math" from, which denotes, "the mental effort needed to think something through." To disciple someone means to help someone progressively learn the Word of God and practically live it out in everyday life. It has been defined as "to train in the truths of Scripture and in the lifestyle required to live these truths out." So, becoming a disciple occurs through belief that leads to behavior.

The third verb is "baptizing." This is found in the following form: present active participle that is plural. Unlike the aorist passive form of "going", baptizing is in the present active tense. They are both participles, but baptizing is the present tense activity of "making disciples." "Having gone, make disciples by baptizing people in the name of the Father, and of the Son, and of the Holy Spirit." Remember, baptizing is the beginning part of the process of discipleship, not the ending point.

The last verb is "teaching." This is in the same exact tense as "baptizing." The New Testament word is "*didasko*" and means "to cause to learn." When it is found in the Bible, it almost always refers to the teaching of Scripture. "Teaching them to obey everything I have commanded you." The word for obey is found 71 times in Scripture and 48 of those times it is translated "keep." We are to teach people to keep the commands of God.

When is the last time you heard a preacher speak on the commands of God? Most of the Lord's Church is not living out His Great Commission. Very few churches have an intentional process to make disciples. And very few pastors teach the commands of Christ found in Scripture.

Double Down on Discipleship

If you take the main verb, "Make disciples" along with the supporting command, "teaching them everything

I commanded you," – you have what I call a "double down on discipleship." "Make disciples" is the divine demand. If we teach His commands, "Make disciples" is one of those commands to be taught. In fact, you could say that making disciples is a great command because it comes in The Great Commission. As you obey His statement to teach His commands, how can you not teach His greatest one? So, there is a two-fold emphasis found in the Great Commission to make disciples. Since Christ came at it from two directions in His commission, let's double down on it as His disciples!

Chapter 3

Discipleship Defined

If discipleship is hitting the spiritual bullseye for the believer, then defining the target is essential. The problem is that so many Christians have a different idea of what discipleship is according to Scripture. Many believers feel they are being discipled if they show up to a weekend worship service or Bible study. Many others feel that discipleship is a private matter that can be done completely alone. Still others feel that discipleship can be done in large groups. None of these ideas mirror the approach Jesus used with His first disciples.

The word "disciple" shows up 261 times in the New Testament. It is found only in five books of the Bible: Each of the Gospels and the book of Acts. This term appears 78 times in the Gospel of John and 72 times in the book of Matthew. This word is mentioned so many times during the life of Jesus, yet most present-day followers of Jesus can't agree on what it actually means.

If we don't know what we are aiming at, how will we know if we ever hit the target when it comes to making disciples? Zig Ziglar once said, "You can't hit a target you cannot see, and you cannot see a target that you do not have."[1]

This statement rings true for so many churches and Christ-followers.

Therefore, we need a definition so that we can have a destination. If we have a purpose, maybe we can see the process to achieve it. If we can put the target up for discipleship, we can aim for all that God has for us.

The following is my biblical definition for discipleship.

**"Discipleship is the intentional process
whereby forgiven people
become faithful followers of Jesus Christ
who bear much fruit."**

This definition reveals a three-fold process and description of discipleship: Forgiven, Following, and Fruitful.

1. Forgiven

The path of discipleship begins with a genuine commitment of faith that leads to the forgiveness of sins. The path of discipleship starts the moment of salvation.

Romans 10:9-10, 13
⁹ If you declare with your mouth, "Jesus is Lord," and believe in your heart that God raised Him from the dead, you will be saved. ¹⁰ For it is with your heart that you believe and are justified, and it is with your mouth that you profess your faith and are saved . . . ¹³ for, "Everyone who calls on the name of the Lord will be saved."

After we call on Him for forgiveness of sins, we then commit to follow Him. This next statement may startle you, but don't stop until you have finished the whole sentence.

It is not God's will that you just become a Christian; it is God's will that you become a fully devoted follower of Jesus Christ. God wants your decision in Him to lead you to becoming a disciple for Him. He wants to move you "From Decision to Discipleship." Since we put our faith in Him for salvation, we follow Him for sanctification. The faith that forever saves is the same faith that daily sustains.

2. Following

We live in a world full of people who have made a decision to believe in Jesus, but have never made a commitment to follow Him. This is nowhere close to what the Bible teaches. All throughout Scripture you will find forgiven people following Jesus.

Matthew 4:19-20
19 "Come, follow Me," Jesus said, "and I will send you out to fish for people." 20 At once they left their nets and followed Him.

It takes more than a decision to become a disciple. There must be a daily commitment in the life of a believer to follow Jesus in order for discipleship to take place. A careful study of Jesus' words from the four Gospels verifies this biblical truth. Jesus told His disciples 5 times, "believe in Me." However, He challenged them 20 times with the statement, "Follow Me."

Jesus said "Follow Me" because He knew where He was going, and He knew where He came from. He left His throne room in Glory to come to earth. He died for our sins and rose again on the third day. He then ascended back to the throne room and is seated at the right hand of God. Thus, He came from Heaven to earth so that He could make a way for us to go from earth to Heaven! He made a way because He is the way! So, we follow Him. John 14:6 teaches that Jesus is the only way to the Father. It is imperative that we follow Him. A commitment to faithfully follow Jesus leads to a fruitful life.

3. Fruitful

For the first disciples, following Jesus led to fishing for men. Followers fish. Truly forgiven people follow Jesus. Following Jesus leads to fruitful lives. This is actually what Jesus taught His first disciples.

John 15:8
This is to My Father's glory, that you bear much fruit, showing yourselves to be My disciples.

One way we show the world that we are disciples of Jesus is by bearing much fruit in our spiritual lives. God's goal for His children is to grow spiritually. As we grow in discipleship, the fruit of the Spirit becomes more evident in our lives. (See Galatians 5:22-23.)

The Apostle Paul taught fruit-bearing as a natural byproduct of belonging to Jesus Christ.

Romans 7:4
So, my brothers and sisters, you also died to the law through the body of Christ, that you might belong to another, to Him who was raised from the dead, in order that we might bear fruit for God.

John the Baptist challenged the religious leaders with a profound truth about discipleship. A decision for Christ through repentance directly correlates to fruit produced in the life of a believer.

Matthew 3:8
Produce fruit in keeping with repentance.

In other words, if you say you have repented of your sins, show it by the spiritual fruit that is produced in your life. Turning from your sins back to your Savior produces good things in the life of a Christ-follower.

The only way to strengthen any discipline, whether it be physical or spiritual, is practice. Every great athlete knows the saying, "Hard work beats talent when talent doesn't work hard." We have also grown up with the saying, "Practice makes perfect." Since nobody's perfect except Jesus, that saying needs to be rewritten. In fact, one of the godliest men I know, Dr. Ronnie Kent, gave me this next statement. This saying is biblically accurate and extremely profound.

"Practice makes Progress; Jesus makes Perfect."

It is our responsibility to discipline ourselves. Since God is perfect, only He can bring our lives to completion. Thus, we practice spiritual disciplines for progress, and Jesus takes that progress and presents us as faultless before the Father.

Hebrews 10:14
For by one sacrifice He has made perfect forever those who are being made holy.

Hebrews 12:11
No discipline seems pleasant at the time, but painful. Later on, however, it produces a harvest of righteousness and peace for those who have been trained by it.

1 Timothy 4:7b-10
[7] ... rather, train yourself to be godly. [8] For physical training is of some value, but godliness has value for all things, holding promise for both the present life and the life to come. [9] This is a trustworthy saying that deserves full acceptance. [10] That is why we labor and strive, because we have put our hope in the living God, who is the Savior of all people, and especially of those who believe.

You put your faith in Jesus at the moment of salvation; now you must follow Jesus in the journey towards discipleship. A decision is made in a moment, but a disciple doesn't just happen in the meantime. The path to discipleship takes sacrifice, dedication, and perseverance. Discipleship is an intentional process. You will not become a disciple by just showing up to church and calling yourself a Christian. Followers of Jesus Christ are not developed overnight. You can't rush discipleship. It's a process that takes time, but you can become a disciple of Jesus Christ. Jesus would never command you to make disciples without enabling you to become one. He has the power to forgive you and develop you into Christ-followers who live fruitful lives.

Chapter 4

The Hinge of Discipleship

There is a new fad going around the decorating world. Old doors that don't have hinges. Antique doors that just lean against walls or stand in open spaces. These doors don't serve the purpose of a door. They don't open and close. They don't connect to the door frame. These doors don't allow entrance from one room to another. These doors are merely for style and not substance. They are for fashion and serve no function.

The true purpose of doors are protection and passageways. They offer protection to keep something dangerous outside from getting inside. That's why many of them have locks on them. Doors also allow pathways from one room to another. As doors swing open, people can enter new areas and move forward in their everyday journeys.

The Bible has a lot of discussion about doorways!

John 10:7, 9 (ESV)
7 So Jesus again said to them, "Truly, truly, I say to you, I am the door of the sheep. . . 9 I am the door. If anyone enters by me, he will be saved and will go in and out and find pasture."

Jesus is the doorway to salvation. As a good shepherd would lay in the entrance to a cave to protect his sheepfold, Jesus, the Good Shepherd, gave His life for His sheep.

Acts 14:27-28

[27] On arriving there, they gathered the church together and reported all that God had done through them and how He had opened a door of faith to the Gentiles. [28] And they stayed there a long time with the disciples.

Acts 14 described the door of faith that God had opened to the Gentiles. The early disciples ministered through this open door of opportunity. As a Gentile, I am glad that door was opened and that the disciples walked through it!

Psalm 24:7

[7] Lift up your heads, you gates; be lifted up, you ancient doors, that the King of glory may come in.

This Psalm depicts the antiphonal praise that was displayed when the victorious army of Israel came back into the city gates. As women and children lifted up their heads and saw their returning husbands and fathers, they celebrated life and victory. As we lift up our heads and expect our returning Savior, we celebrate resurrection power and the eternal victory that comes through being a child of God. The King of glory enters ancient doors!

Matthew 7:7-8

[7] "Ask and it will be given to you; seek and you will find; knock and the door will be opened to you. [8] For everyone who asks receives; the one who seeks finds; and to the one who knocks, the door will be opened."

Through our prayer life as a believer, God can open doors. We just need to keep on knocking and seeking, so that we will find Him faithful to enter every area of our lives and open the doors to those who need to be discipled.

Revelation 3:7-8
[7] "To the angel of the church in Philadelphia write:
These are the words of Him who is holy and true, who holds the key of David. What He opens no one can shut, and what He shuts no one can open. [8] I know your deeds. See, I have placed before you an open door that no one can shut. I know that you have little strength, yet you have kept My word and have not denied My name.

Jesus is King and He holds the keys to the kingdom. When He opens a door, no one can shut it. And when He closes doors, no one can open them. God has placed before His church an open door that no one can shut. As His children, it is our duty to obey the commission and command of Christ. Our role is to walk through the open door.

The church today has been given a doorway to become followers of Jesus Christ, but it has been unhinged and propped up as a mere fad in most of our churches. Discipleship is something that is hardly talked about, much less practiced.

- What if the doorway to all that God has for us hinges on discipleship?
- What if the entranceway to live out His Word is directly connected to discipleship?
- What if the only way to be all that He called us to be is to obey all that He called us to do?

Perhaps a picture God revealed to me will make discipleship clearer.

I call this diagram "The Hinge of Discipleship." The wall and the door frame are the Word of God. God's Word frames everything He wants for His children. The door itself is God's will for your life and mine. When believers live out God's will, the church fulfills its purpose! The hinge is discipleship! Discipleship is what connects God's Word to His will for your life!

Unlike the doors of fashion and fad today, the hinge is essential to join all that God says in His Word to all that He has called us to be as His followers!

Standard doors and sliding doors only open one way. (Now saloon doors open two ways because as soon as you make a mistake and go in, you should turn around and leave. That's another book for another day!) Most doors only open one way. There is only one way to be all that God has created us to be. God created us and then He wrote the Book! God made us in His image and then gave us the Instruction Manual. God gave us His Spirit and then He gave us Scripture. It is in that order for a reason! When we do it His way, we become all that He wants us to be. We get His Plan A when we follow His prescription for the Christian life! Discipleship is God's Plan A for His creation. He has no Plan B. He is the way, the truth, and the life! We must follow His way and obey His truth, so that we can find the meaning and purpose of life!

There is one more thing God revealed to me about the "Hinge of Discipleship." You can only see the hinge when the door is open. When the door is closed, hinges are hidden. But when the door is open wide, the hinges are most visible. If we want God to swing the door of opportunity wide open for His church, we need to get back to a clear focus on discipleship!

Chapter 5

The Model for Making Disciples

The perfect model for discipleship is Jesus with His first disciples. Jesus spent intimate time with His twelve disciples. Christ spent even more time bonding with the inner circle of Peter, James, and John. If you study the Gospels, you will discover that Jesus was with large crowds on 17 occasions, but He spent time with small groups of people 46 times. Jesus wasn't into building crowds; He was focused on making disciples. And Jesus knows that the only way to make disciples is through meaningful, personal, and intimate relationships. Therefore, Jesus called His disciples and taught them consistently. The disciples watched Jesus live life in front of them as the model of spiritual maturity. Jesus developed them and equipped them. Then He deployed them into the world and entrusted ministry to them. So how did Jesus do with those first disciples? I would say He discipled them so well, that after He died, rose again, and descended to the Father; they gave their lives for the Gospel and turned the world upside down for Jesus. Most leaders in today's church can't convince Christians to go to church. These first disciples came to Christ and then committed their lives to the cause!

The next best model of discipleship is the first disciples and the early church. I mean, Jesus is a hard act to follow! He is perfect and they were converted blue collar workers. The real test would be if the Lord's first disciples could take the model from Jesus and make discipleship work as the Gospel spread.

The book of Acts tells us how these first disciples faired at making disciples. It wouldn't be easy. They had obstacles and problems everywhere. Persecution of Christians was rampant. Jesus had been crucified, which put fear into all that would associate with His name! Then there was the sheer magnitude of the task at hand. Have you ever heard someone in church leadership say, "We just grew too fast to have time to make disciples."? Well take a look at all the early church overcame in order to make disciples.

In Acts 1, Jesus told His disciples to wait in Jerusalem and He promised them the Holy Spirit would come. Waiting was their first test. Do you know of anyone on the planet that likes to wait? I mean, just a few verses later, they ask Him about the timing of everything! Jesus' response in Acts 1:7 was short and to the point. Jesus basically said, "My Father sets the time and you don't need to know when." These first disciples had to trust that if God said it, that settles it! His Word was all that they needed as instructions.

Then Jesus gave His disciples another set of marching orders.

Act 1:8
8 But you will receive power when the Holy Spirit comes on you; and you will be My witnesses in Jerusalem, and in all Judea and Samaria, and to the ends of the earth."

Jesus basically moved them in their thinking from worrying about *when*, to focusing on *Who* will be with them each step of the journey. We get so caught up in times and places that we miss His truth and the power of the Holy Spirit that's all around us.

Then, Jesus ascends into Heaven before their very eyes. God sends two angels to challenge them on why they were just standing there looking up into the sky. They told the disciples that Jesus will come back the same way He went up. Translation, "Get to work guys. Quit standing around. He's coming back one day!"

So, the disciples obey the word of the Lord and go back to Jerusalem. They went to the Upper Room and joined together constantly in prayer. Then Peter got up in front of the group that had gathered and quoted Scripture from Psalm 69:25 and Psalm 109:8. About 120 people were present. This resulted in Matthias being added to the eleven disciples to replace the spot left open by Judas.

Acts 2 opens up with Pentecost! The Holy Spirit that Jesus had promised in Acts 1 falls on the people. Then Peter gets up and preaches. Peter's sermon is recorded in Acts 2:14-41. During his sermon, he quotes from Joel 2, Psalm 16, and Psalm 110. In the Psalm 16 passage, Peter quotes from David. It is recorded in Acts 2:28.

Acts 2:28

"You have made known to me the paths of life; You will fill me with joy in Your presence."

Peter reminded the crowd of what David knew. That God has a path of life for us to travel. And there is joy in the presence of the Lord as we live the life He has called us to. This is an incredible discipleship verse. When we follow His will, He fills us with the joy of Himself! We know through His Word that His will is for us to be discipled and to make disciples. We will never have more peace than when we are maturing as His disciples and on mission to make disciples.

Peter then continues to preach the death, burial, and resurrection of Jesus. He calls for people to repent and be baptized. And 3,000 people were saved and added to the church that day! God can do more in a day than we can do in a lifetime! I would love to have been in that worship service! The Holy Spirit falls and Peter preaches, and thousands are saved! Talk about fast church growth. How do you deal with 3000 additions in one day?

Acts 2 ends with a description of how the church lived out their faith! It is not a program, but these verses do reveal God's plan for His church. It is how the early church made disciples! Some church leaders get five focuses of the early church from these verses: Worship, Evangelism, Discipleship, Fellowship, and Ministry. I have outlined the verses that speak to each one of these five areas.

Acts 2:42-47

42 They devoted themselves to the apostles' teaching and to fellowship, to the breaking of bread and to prayer. 43 Everyone was filled with awe at the many wonders and signs performed by the apostles. 44 All the believers were together and had everything in common. 45 They sold property and possessions to give to anyone who had need. 46 Every day they continued to meet together in the temple courts. They broke bread in their homes and ate together with glad and sincere hearts, 47 praising God and enjoying the favor of all the people. And the Lord added to their number daily those who were being saved.

Worship	vs. 43	Everyone was filled with awe at the many wonders and signs performed by the apostles.
	vs. 47	praising God . . .
Evangelism	vs. 47	And the Lord added to their number daily those who were being saved.
Discipleship	vs. 42	devoted themselves to the apostles teaching, . . . and to prayer
Fellowship	vs. 42	. . . and to fellowship, to the breaking of bread. . .
	vs. 44	All the believers were together and had everything in common.
	vs. 46	Every day they continued to meet together in the temple courts. They broke bread in their homes and ate together with glad and sincere hearts.
Ministry	vs. 45	They sold their property and possessions to give to anyone who had a need.

This was the model for discipleship for the early church. And it worked! 3000 people got saved to start the process. As the early church focused on relationships for discipleship, the

Lord continued to add "to their number daily those who were being saved."

We will come back and talk about the verses that have been denoted as discipleship from Acts 2:42 in the next few chapters. I personally don't see discipleship as one of the five areas. I believe discipleship is the process and the byproduct of the other four areas along with Bible study and prayer. That is a discussion for another chapter.

Just know that Jesus modeled discipleship perfectly to His first disciples. These disciples modeled it to the early church. And the early church would model it to the world. Disciples were being made who, in turn, made disciples.

They weren't focused on church growth. They focused on making disciples and trusted Jesus to grow His church. Maybe our focus is all wrong. Maybe we are too focused on attracting crowds that we aren't making disciples. Maybe we are too focused on the traditional order of church: Getting people into worship services, then Bible Studies, and then hopefully people will get into smaller groups for discipleship. When Jesus and the first disciples had this order: They made disciples by teaching the Word of God and the result was that people worshipped God!

Well, I would argue that what we are doing isn't working for making disciples. We need a model that will move people from making decisions to becoming disciples. Since it was Jesus who gave us the divine demand, shouldn't we go with His plan for discipleship?

Chapter 6

Two Weapons for Disciple-Making

The previous chapter included a breakdown of Acts 2:42-47 into five areas of focus for the early church. These five areas were made popular by Rick Warren's book *"Purpose Driven Church."* They are: Worship, Evangelism, Discipleship, Fellowship, and Ministry.[1] These have been referred by others under headings such as "The Five Purposes of the Church" and "The Five Dimensions of a Healthy Church." While we will discuss my thoughts on these areas in the second half of this book, I want to focus on Discipleship in this chapter from that common breakdown of the five purposes of the church.

If you divide each of those five areas out from the text in Acts 2, as we did in the last chapter, what you have left for discipleship is as follows:

Discipleship   vs. 42   devoted themselves to the
                              apostles teaching, ...and to prayer

Isn't it interesting that what we have left from Acts 2:42-47 are the only two offensive weapons found in the armor of God mentioned in Ephesians 6:10-18? I know what some of you are thinking. You are saying to yourself right now,

38

"There is only one offensive weapon and that is the Word of God." Oh, but I beg to differ. I believe there is one more offensive weapon – prayer! Let's study Ephesians 6 and see what the Word says.

Ephesians 6:10-14a
[10] Finally, be strong in the Lord and in His mighty power. [11] Put on the full armor of God, so that you can take your stand against the devil's schemes. [12] For our struggle is not against flesh and blood, but against the rulers, against the authorities, against the powers of this dark world and against the spiritual forces of evil in the heavenly realms. [13] Therefore put on the full armor of God, so that when the day of evil comes, you may be able to stand your ground, and after you have done everything, to stand. [14] Stand firm then, . . .

Verse 10 teaches that our strength comes from the Lord. His mighty power is the source of our strength for all spiritual battles. The Lord provides the power for the struggle. Verse 11 tells us specifically to "put on the full armor of God." Scripture re-emphasizes this a second time in verse 13. This means that every single piece of armor is not only important, but essential. We can't go into our daily battles without being fully equipped for the fight. Verse 12 states the place of our struggle. Our battle is in the unseen realm against the devil and all his forces of evil.

Four times in verses 10-14a we see the word "stand." Therefore, the Scripture begins with "be strong" and then repeatedly says, "stand." There is no retreat in the Christian's playbook. As many Bible teachers have noted, there is no piece of armor for your backside. You fight the battle against the devil by standing tall and fighting in the strength of the

Lord. As my grandfather used to always say, "You either face the devil every single day, or you're both headed in the same direction." This is a toe-to-toe and face-to-face battle. Then, each piece of the armor of God is mentioned.

Ephesians 6:14-17
14 Stand firm then, with the belt of truth buckled around your waist, with the breastplate of righteousness in place, 15 and with your feet fitted with the readiness that comes from the gospel of peace. 16 In addition to all this, take up the shield of faith, with which you can extinguish all the flaming arrows of the evil one. 17 Take the helmet of salvation and the sword of the Spirit, which is the Word of God.

The armor for the believer is as follows: belt of truth, breastplate of righteousness, feet fitted with the readiness of the Gospel, shield of faith, helmet of salvation, and the Sword of the Spirit, which is the Word of God. In this list, everything is defensive except the Word of God. One might say, "Well a sword can be used for offensive and defensive purposes." Perhaps a closer look at the New Testament word for "sword" in this verse will enlighten us. The word used for "sword" in Ephesians 6:17 is the Greek word "***machaira***." This was a short sword or dagger mainly used for stabbing in biblical times. It is defined as "a slaughter knife" and it was the weapon of choice for taking vengeance or exacting retribution. This is the same word for sword mentioned in the following verses. In fact, every time you read the word "sword" in these next six references, it is the short thrusting sword "***machaira***."

Matthew 10:34
"Do not suppose that I have come to bring peace to the earth. I did not come to bring peace, but a sword."

Matthew 26:47-55

⁴⁷ While He was still speaking, Judas, one of the Twelve, arrived. With him was a large crowd armed with swords and clubs, sent from the chief priests and the elders of the people. ⁴⁸ Now the betrayer had arranged a signal with them: "The one I kiss is the man; arrest Him." ⁴⁹ Going at once to Jesus, Judas said, "Greetings, Rabbi!" and kissed Him. ⁵⁰ Jesus replied, "Do what you came for, friend." Then the men stepped forward, seized Jesus and arrested Him. ⁵¹ With that, one of Jesus' companions reached for his sword, drew it out and struck the servant of the high priest, cutting off his ear. ⁵² "Put your sword back in its place," Jesus said to him, "for all who draw the sword will die by the sword. ⁵³ Do you think I cannot call on My Father, and He will at once put at My disposal more than twelve legions of angels? ⁵⁴ But how then would the Scriptures be fulfilled that say it must happen in this way?" ⁵⁵ In that hour Jesus said to the crowd, "Am I leading a rebellion, that you have come out with swords and clubs to capture Me? Every day I sat in the temple courts teaching, and you did not arrest Me."

Luke 21:24

²⁴ They will fall by the sword and will be taken as prisoners to all the nations. Jerusalem will be trampled on by the Gentiles until the times of the Gentiles are fulfilled.

Acts 12:2

He had James, the brother of John, put to death with the sword.

Romans 8:35

Who shall separate us from the love of Christ? Shall trouble or hardship or persecution or famine or nakedness or danger or sword?

Hebrews 4:12
For the word of God is alive and active. Sharper than any double-edged sword, it penetrates even to dividing soul and spirit, joints and marrow; it judges the thoughts and attitudes of the heart.

Make no mistake, the Sword of the Spirit that is the Word of God is a powerful offensive weapon in the hands of the believer.

The problem with most studies on the armor of God is they stop short of the last offensive weapon.

Ephesians 6:18-20
[18] And pray in the Spirit on all occasions with all kinds of prayers and requests. With this in mind, be alert and always keep on praying for all the Lord's people. [19] Pray also for me, that whenever I speak, words may be given me so that I will fearlessly make known the mystery of the gospel, [20] for which I am an ambassador in chains. Pray that I may declare it fearlessly, as I should.

The first word in verse 18 is extremely important. It is not the word "and" like you would think. That is the way translators worded it in the English to form a new sentence for readability. It is actually the Greek word *"dia"* which means "through." In the language of the New Testament, verse 17 begins a new sentence that does not stop until the end of verse 20. Scripture actually teaches that we take the helmet of salvation and the sword of the spirit "through all prayer and supplication." Prayer is another part of the armor of God. And I believe it is the second offensive weapon.

Six times in verses 18-20, Paul uses a term for prayer. The main verb for prayer is the first one found in verse 18. "And pray in the Spirit on all occasions with all kinds of prayer." That first word "pray" is translated from the Greek word "***proseuche***." It comes from the following two Greek words: "***pros***" meaning "towards" and "***euche***" meaning "a prayer comprising a vow." This word means "toward a commitment in prayer." This word is actually found twice in Ephesians 6:18. I have noted them for you below.

Ephesians 6:18
*And **pray** in the Spirit on all occasions with all kinds of **prayers** and requests.*

This is the same word that Matthew, Mark, and Luke all chose to record Jesus' rebuke of the money changers in the Temple. In this rebuke, Jesus quoted from Isaiah 56:7 and Jeremiah 7:11. Here is how Matthew states it in his Gospel.

Matthew 21:13
"It is written," He said to them, "'My house will be called a house of prayer,' but you are making it 'a den of robbers.'"

Jesus called His house a dedicated place of prayer. Christ-followers are the temple of the Holy Spirit of God. The power of the Holy Spirit lives in each disciple of Jesus Christ. Like His Temple in Matthew 21:13, our bodies should house a devoted prayer life. A committed prayer life is a powerful offensive weapon in our daily spiritual warfare.

Ephesians 6:18 contains one more word for prayer. It is the Greek word, "***deesis***." It is a word that means "a heartfelt petition" and is translated "petition, request, or supplication." This word also occurs twice in this verse. Therefore, twice we have the word for "a commitment to prayer" and twice we have the word for "praying for others." A serious commitment to pray for and with each other is a great tool for discipleship.

Therefore, a devotion to the apostles teaching (the study of God's Word) and prayer are the two offensive weapons for disciple-making. In fact, you will discover in the next chapter how these two spiritual disciplines connect everything together in the intentional process of discipleship.

It is impossible to take your stand and fight off the adversary without a commitment to God's Word and prayer. We will never be able to grow as disciples of Jesus Christ without a proper understanding and application of His Word. Since communication is the key component in any relationship, our development as disciples will always be directly proportional to our dedication to prayer. How can we commit ourselves to be followers of Jesus Christ if we don't devote ourselves to speaking and listening to Him on a regular basis? Let's be strong and stand firm! Armor up! Take your offensive weapons with you and let's mature as disciples and let's make disciples!

Chapter 7

A Discipleship Revolution

As we stated earlier, most church leaders list the five purposes of the church as follows: Worship, Evangelism, Discipleship, Fellowship, and Ministry. I am definitely not advocating that these are not the purposes of the church. However, I do not believe that just offering church programs categorized under these five headings will turn people into fully devoted disciples of Jesus Christ. What if the church viewed these as five aspects of a disciple's life? You don't go to worship, program evangelism, plan discipleship, have a fellowship time, and do ministry. Rather, your passion is Jesus, your burden is for the lost, you want to follow Jesus and mature, you know you can't do it alone, and you are overjoyed that you get to serve Jesus.

I do not believe that Acts 2:42-47 was recorded in Scripture to give us our church programs. Neither do I believe that you can program discipleship. I do believe that there must be a clear intentional path for discipleship provided and encouraged by God's church. These verses in Acts 2 were given as a description of the first church and as a picture for all future churches. I was in a discipleship conference and overheard this profound statement:

"Jesus started the church the way He wanted it! Now, He wants it the way He started it!" God does have a plan for His church. His plan is for His church to make disciples.

Is it possible that we have erred in our past approach to discipleship? In the past, many scholars have approached discipleship as one spoke in the wheel of Christlikeness. What if discipleship is the whole wheel? What if discipleship is not a part of the process, but the entire purpose of the process? Isn't discipleship the end product of the church? What if worship, evangelism, fellowship, and ministry were all parts of what it means to become a disciple of Jesus Christ? What if the two offensive weapons of Bible study and prayer are what connects all of these parts?

Just maybe we need a transformation in our concept of discipleship. Perhaps we need a revolution in our thinking concerning discipleship. This following diagram is what I call "A Discipleship Revolution."

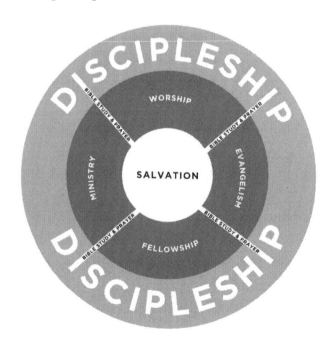

Paul includes the Word of God and prayer as the offensive weapons for the believer for a specific reason. These two tools connect everything together for the life of a believer. Bible study and prayer also form the foundation for worship, evangelism, fellowship, and ministry. Each of these four areas in the life of a Christ-follower must be informed by Scripture and empowered by prayer. From the point of salvation, these four areas, along with Bible study and prayer, move the believer towards discipleship. Discipleship is developed through biblical worship, evangelism, fellowship, and ministry. The by-product of a life prayerfully committed to these four areas culminates in believers becoming disciples of Jesus Christ.

The early church devoted themselves to these purposes.

Acts 2:42
They devoted themselves to the apostles' teaching and to fellowship, to the breaking of bread and to prayer.

The word for "devoted" in Acts 2:42 is a word that is sometimes translated, "steadfastly continued." It comes from the compound New Testament word, "*proskartereo*." The first part comes from the word "*pros*" which means "towards" or "with." The second part is the Greek word "*kartereo*," which means, "to show steadfast strength." This word comes from the New Testament word "*kratos*," a term meaning, "prevailing strength." Biblehub.com defines this word devoted as, "to continue to do something with intense effort despite difficulty." In other words, no matter what happens around you, keep your commitment to these areas with determination and perseverance with unyielding strength.

This is the same word used in Acts 2:46 and also back in Acts 1:14. It occurs again in Acts 6:4. I have underlined the word in each of the following Scriptures.

Acts 2:46
*Every day **they continued** to meet together in the temple courts. They broke bread in their homes and ate together with glad and sincere hearts,*

Acts 1:14
*They **all joined together constantly** in prayer, along with the women and Mary the mother of Jesus, and with His brothers.*

Acts 6:4
*and **will give our attention** to prayer and the ministry of the word."*

Paul uses this same word with an emphasis on prayer to the church at Colossae.

Colossians 4:2
Devote yourselves *to prayer, being watchful and thankful.*

Did you notice how many times the word for "devoted" found in Acts 2:42 shows up elsewhere in Scripture concerning prayer? These early believers were steadfastly praying and studying God's Word. The reason the early church did such an awesome job at making disciples is because they were devoted to obeying Christ's command to "make disciples."

These early Christians faced intense persecution. Yet, they did not allow anything to detour them or distract them from completing the task that God had commanded of them.

Our society today is distracted by so many things. Cultural conformity and complacency have found their way into the church. We devote ourselves so much to social media, sports, occupations, and the pursuit of possessions, that we are too busy to obey the most important commandment that God has called us to. God's command to His church is still to "make disciples."

Let's look at one more place where the term "***proskartereo***" or "devoted" is recorded in the book of Acts.

Acts 8:13
Simon himself believed and was baptized. And **he followed** *Philip* **everywhere***, astonished by the great signs and miracles he saw.*

In Acts 8, Philip had gone down to the city of Samaria and preached the Good News of Jesus Christ. A very popular man in that city was named Simon. He had practiced sorcery and led many people astray. But when Simon heard the Gospel proclaimed by Philip, he trusted in Jesus Christ for salvation and was baptized. Verse 13 of Acts 8 states that after Simon was saved, he followed Philip everywhere. That phrase, "he followed everywhere" is the same word used in Acts 2:42 where the early Christians "devoted themselves to the apostles teaching and prayer." Simon devoted himself to following Philip everywhere Philip went. Philip discipled Simon and Simon steadfastly devoted himself to the journey of discipleship! This is a great lesson on how devotion to God's Word and prayer connects to a commitment to following Christian mentors in a continual process of discipleship.

These early Christians lived simple lives sold out to their Savior. Many of us today live complicated lives sold out to the world. We need an uprising in the church in the area of discipleship. The church needs a call back to their commitment to Christ. Those of us called by His name must have "A Discipleship Revolution."

Chapter 8

Worship - The Disciple's Passion

As we reflect on moving people from making a decision to maturing as a disciple, we need to look closer at how each of the five major purposes of the church function to facilitate discipleship. It is what I call, "**The Daily Development of a Disciple's Life.**"

Discipleship is a journey that takes time. The fulfilled life of a disciple comes from daily development. Discipleship is a daily step closer to Jesus that results from a five-fold focus. Acts 2:42-47 identify five specific characteristics of His church.

Acts 2:42-47
42 They devoted themselves to the apostles' teaching and to fellowship, to the breaking of bread and to prayer. 43 Everyone was filled with awe at the many wonders and signs performed by the apostles. 44 All the believers were together and had everything in common. 45 They sold property and possessions to give to anyone who had need. 46 Every day they continued to meet together in the temple courts. They broke bread in their homes and ate together with glad and sincere hearts, 47 praising God and enjoying the favor of all the people. And the Lord added to their number daily those who were being saved.

The Daily Development of a Disciple's Life

W	**"Worship"**	**The Disciple's Passion**
E	**"Evangelism"**	**The Disciple's Purpose**
D	**"Discipleship"**	**The Disciple's Path**
F	**"Fellowship"**	**The Disciple's Partnership**
M	**"Ministry"**	**The Disciple's Posture**

Remember, these are not five parts of a program. You cannot program discipleship. Discipleship is the byproduct of the whole process and the ultimate purpose of the church for every believer. However, each one of these biblical areas impact the process of discipleship.

In the next 5 chapters, we will deal with each one of these characteristics from the early church. But just to clarify, the discussion of this entire book is about making disciples. The conversation in Chapter 10 will be about becoming a disciple. Before we can make disciples, we have to be on the journey to becoming one ourselves.

The section of Acts 2:42-47 that deals with worship is as follows:

Acts 2:43, 47
⁴³ Everyone was filled with awe at the many wonders and signs performed by the apostles. ⁴⁷ praising God and enjoying the favor of all the people. . .

Worship is a part of becoming a disciple of Jesus. It is also a byproduct of discipleship. In other words, worshipping God helps us grow in our walk with the Lord. Yet the flip side of the coin is that growing disciples desire to worship Jesus. The more you mature as a disciple, the more you want to worship the Savior you are following.

Jesus gave priority to worship when He gave the Greatest Commandment.

Matthew 22:36-40

[36] "Teacher, which is the greatest commandment in the Law?" [37] Jesus replied: "'Love the Lord your God with all your heart and with all your soul and with all your mind.' [38] This is the first and greatest commandment. [39] And the second is like it: 'Love your neighbor as yourself.' [40] All the Law and the Prophets hang on these two commandments."

Every command of the law and every word from the prophets connect to two principles: Loving God and loving your neighbor as yourself. You can hang every Word of God on the hook of your love for Him. The greatest privilege we have is to worship God for who He is and for all He's done. Worship comes from a deep-rooted love relationship with your Lord and Savior!

In order to understand how worship connects to discipleship, we need a good working definition. Of all the definitions I have ever heard on worship, my favorite is from pastor, mentor, and friend – Pastor Rick Ousley. He defines worship as follows:

**"Worship is our response to God
for who He is and what He has done,
expressed in the things we say
and the way we live."[1]**

52

First of all, **worship is a response**. Notice Isaiah's response to being in the presence of God.

Isaiah 6:1, 5
¹ In the year that King Uzziah died, I saw the Lord, high and exalted, seated on a throne; and the train of His robe filled the temple. . . ⁵ "Woe to me!" I cried. "I am ruined! For I am a man of unclean lips, and I live among a people of unclean lips, and my eyes have seen the King, the Lord Almighty."

When Isaiah saw the Lord for who He is, he also saw himself for who he was. Everything about God is holy. We are all unholy. When we see Jesus high and lifted up, we see ourselves as lowly in comparison. Worship involves a response to experiencing God.

One pastor expressed worship as, "The rhythm of revelation and response."[2] God reveals Himself and we respond, much like Isaiah did in the above Scripture. There are also examples, such as 1 Kings 18:38-39, when God reveals Himself and the people responded by immediately going facedown.

1 Kings 18:38-39
³⁸ Then the fire of the Lord fell and burned up the sacrifice, the wood, the stones and the soil, and also licked up the water in the trench. ³⁹ When all the people saw this, they fell prostrate and cried, "The Lord—He is God! The Lord—He is God!"

Bowing down with our faces flat on the ground is an appropriate response when we realize who God is. And in the previous Scripture in 1 Kings 18, those who responded were pagan worshippers. If lost people can respond to God when

He reveals Himself, how much more should we worship God as His followers?

And notice from the definition of worship that we respond to all that God is and what He has done. When things don't go our way and trials invade, many times we stop worshipping God. But God doesn't owe us anything. And isn't Calvary enough? Isn't who He is more than enough reason for us to worship Him?!

Secondly, **worship is a verb**. Worship involves action. Worship is not just something we talk about; it is something we are involved in. Listen to the actions of worship described by David in the Psalms and Paul to the church at Rome.

Psalm 96:8-9

[8] Ascribe to the LORD the glory due His name; bring an offering and come into His courts. [9] Worship the LORD in the splendor of His holiness; tremble before Him, all the earth.

Romans 12:1

Therefore, I urge you, brothers and sisters, in view of God's mercy, to offer your bodies as a living sacrifice, holy and pleasing to God—this is your true and proper worship.

Worship is something you participate in! We worship God by ascribing Him glory, bringing an offering, living holy lives, and trembling before Him.

The previous definition of worship ends with, ". . . **expressed in the things we say and the way we live**." Worship has action to it! We have a problem with that in our culture. Most of us grew up watching worship rather than experiencing God. Many of us also grew up believing that worship was a corporate gathering at an assigned time and place.

Now that we have a good working definition of worship, when does worship take place? When exactly does worship take place in the life of a believer? Do you just turn worship on like a light switch when you come into a church building and have a "worship service?" Well of course not. But we have named the hour on Sunday the "Worship hour." We have called the handout with the announcements, "The Worship Guide." We even label the first part of the church service as the "Worship Time" followed by time in the Word.

Biblically we should be telling believers this next statement often: "We don't come to church to worship; we bring our worship to church!" We can't approach worship like it is something that we do only in a church sanctuary on Sunday morning one hour a week. Many people only worship God in a segment of time labeled as a worship service. What if every Christian truly worshipped God throughout their work week and then all showed up as worshippers to their respective church on the weekend? What would happen if worship became a daily lifestyle and not just a lone event for every believer? Worship was never to be limited to a church building. And the adoration of God was never meant to be something we just do with our mouths.

Biblical worship is an any-moment, every-day privilege for the believer!

First of all, worship can occur at any moment. There is not a moment that goes by that does not contain within it, an opportunity to worship.

Hebrews 13:15-16
[15] Through Jesus, therefore, let us continually offer to God a sacrifice of praise-the fruit of lips that openly profess His name. [16] And do not forget to do good and to share with others, for with such sacrifices God is pleased.

True worship is not just any moment, but it is also every day.

Psalm 145:2
Every day I will praise You, and extol Your name for ever and ever.

Did you notice in the verses the phrases, "continually offer" and "every day?" You can make a daily decision to continually offer God praise by the things you say and the way you live. But worship is a decision you have to make! Worship allows me to connect my personal relationship with God with a passionate response to His greatness. No one can give God your personal worship except you. In fact, did you know that you can give God something that He doesn't already have? I know, you think I'm crazy because God already owns everything, right? But there is one thing that God doesn't have unless you give it to Him. And that is the praise from your lips and the worship of your life. Don't pass up opportunities to bless His name and to worship Him in spirit and in truth. Make a daily decision to devote yourself to the worship of Almighty God.

Deuteronomy 32:3
I will proclaim the name of the LORD. Oh, praise the greatness of our God!

Worship also connects to obedience. Do you know when the word "worship" first shows up in Scripture? It is when Abraham is commanded by God to offer Isaac on an altar of sacrifice. Scripture records Abraham's words in Genesis 22 as follows:

Genesis 22:1-5

¹ Some time later God tested Abraham. He said to him, "Abraham!" "Here I am," he replied. ² Then God said, "Take your son, your only son, whom you love—Isaac—and go to the region of Moriah. Sacrifice him there as a burnt offering on a mountain I will show you." ³ Early the next morning Abraham got up and loaded his donkey. He took with him two of his servants and his son Isaac. When he had cut enough wood for the burnt offering, he set out for the place God had told him about. ⁴ On the third day Abraham looked up and saw the place in the distance. ⁵ He said to his servants, "Stay here with the donkey while I and the boy go over there. We will worship and then we will come back to you."

The first time you read about worship in Scripture, it is tied to obedience and sacrifice. Worship is not just something you do with your lips; it is also something done with your life!

You might be saying, "Well how does worship tie into discipleship?" The answer is simple. You will never devote yourself to following Jesus until you, first of all, love Him deeply. Determination towards a religion grows old quickly. However, dedication to someone you love in a meaningful relationship can last through the worst of circumstances. If you truly love God, you can't help but respond in worship with your words and actions. When you truly love God, you want to obey His commands. You are willing to sacrifice to show your love to Him! True worshippers lead to believers becoming disciples. And the more you learn about who God is through discipleship, the more reasons you have to worship Him. It is a continual circle that grows and matures as you continue to follow Christ in a real and relevant relationship.

The process looks like this: I love God more than anything, so I obey God's command to follow Him. As I follow Him more deeply, I begin to know Him more intimately. Every time God reveals Himself to me, I respond in adoration and praise. There is this constant relationship rhythm where God reveals Himself and I continue responding. The longer I follow Him, the more I learn about Him. The more I learn about Him, the more reasons I have to respond to Him in worship. With a relationship with Jesus like that, nobody has to tell me it is time to stand and worship Him. Nobody has to lead me to worship. God has already led me to Him; and worship is an automatic response of seeing Jesus! You will never grow to be a disciple of Jesus Christ without first having a passion for Him. And you will never have an unbelievable passion for Him that doesn't drive you to want to follow Him more deeply.

One more reason worship is connected to making disciples is that authentic worship transforms the believer. You are drawn closer to Jesus every time you encounter Jesus in worship.

There is an interesting passage of Scripture found in Ezekiel 46. Many theologians believe this is the Temple that will be reconstructed during Jesus' millennial reign. There are some specific and unique descriptions given as to how you enter and exit worship during this new era.

Ezekiel 46:1-2, 8-10

" ¹ This is what the Sovereign Lord says: The gate of the inner court facing east is to be shut on the six working days, but on the Sabbath day and on the day of the New Moon it is to be opened. ² The prince is to enter from the outside through the portico of the gateway and stand by the gatepost. The priests are to sacrifice his burnt offering and his fellowship offerings.

He is to bow down in worship at the threshold of the gateway and then go out, but the gate will not be shut until evening. . . [8] When the prince enters, he is to go in through the portico of the gateway, and he is to come out the same way. [9] "'When the people of the land come before the Lord at the appointed festivals, whoever enters by the north gate to worship is to go out the south gate; and whoever enters by the south gate is to go out the north gate. No one is to return through the gate by which they entered, but each is to go out the opposite gate. [10] The prince is to be among them, going in when they go in and going out when they go out."

The Prince, who is Jesus, comes in and out the same gate. However, the people cannot go out the same gate they came in by. Upon exiting the worship of Jesus, the people must go out a different gate. There is some great theological significance to these interesting details. Why is it so important that Jesus goes in and out the same gate, yet the people must leave worship out of a different gate than the one through which they entered? Jesus comes in and out the same gate because He is always the same. He is the same God yesterday, today, and forever. However, after the people experience God through worship, they are never the same! The fact that people go out a different gate is a picture of how worshipping Jesus forever changes you. You never leave spiritually the same way you came to church when genuine worship takes place. Every time God changes you, He grows you more into the disciple He desires for you to become!

Chapter 9

Evangelism - The Disciple's Purpose

As we continue looking at "**The Daily Development of a Disciple's Life**," let's focus on evangelism. The biblical word "evangelism" comes from the Greek word "*euaggelion*" which means, "a message of good news." The verb form "*euaggelizeo*" means "to announce or preach the Gospel." The word for angel is found in both of those New Testament words. It is the word "*aggelos*." This word for angel can also be translated "messenger." Therefore, a biblical definition of evangelism is "a messenger who announces the Good News of Jesus Christ."

The following is how Acts 2 describes the results of evangelism in the early church:

Acts 2:47
. . . And the Lord added to their number daily those who were being saved.

Discipleship begins and ends with evangelism. Evangelism places a person on the road to discipleship. That road to discipleship leads to evangelism in the life of the believer. Discipleship isn't complete until further

60

evangelism takes place. Evangelism isn't complete until we are disciples. Evangelism is the purpose for every disciple of Jesus Christ.

Mark 16:15
He said to them, "Go into all the world and preach the gospel to all creation."

Matthew 28:19-20
[19] Therefore go and make disciples of all nations, baptizing them in the name of the Father and of the Son and of the Holy Spirit, [20] and teaching them to obey everything I have commanded you. And surely I am with you always, to the very end of the age.

You can't even spell the word Gospel without the word "Go."

By the language of the New Testament, the Great Commission can be translated, "As you are going . . ." In other words, God already expects us to be going and spreading the Good News that Jesus saves! This is the last thing Jesus told His disciples. In Acts 1:8, Jesus tells them, "You will be My witnesses . . ." The last words from Jesus should carry enough weight that we act on them. Ed Stetzer once said, "Many Christians love evangelism as long as someone else is doing it."[1] Are you expecting other people to witness and go, or do you see your responsibility to share the message of Christ?

As we focus on the connection of evangelism to discipleship, this next statement is a good starting place. **"Live Sold Out."** I am sold on the fact that believers should be sold out for Jesus. Jesus gave us His all! Why should we give Him any less in return? It is essential that we carry the Gospel to the world. We wouldn't be believers if someone hadn't told us, and the lost world won't be saved unless someone tells them!

Romans 10:14-15

[14] How, then, can they call on the one they have not believed in? And how can they believe in the one of whom they have not heard? And how can they hear without someone preaching to them? [15] And how can anyone preach unless they are sent? As it is written: "How beautiful are the feet of those who bring good news!"

We need more beautiful feet for Jesus! There is a desperate need for Christians to share their faith.

Jesus paid it all and ascended to Heaven and is sitting at the right hand of the Father. He is watching to see if the saved go in the Holy Spirit's power and become His hands and feet to the world. We have the same mission of our Savior Jesus Christ. Please understand that we cannot save anyone; only Christ can accomplish that. However, Christ speaks and works through His children to spread the Good News. Jesus gives this very important message to His disciples.

Secondly, **"Live Sent."** Research shows that most Christians do not share their faith. Studies indicate that 90 percent of evangelicals have never shared their faith with anyone outside of their family.[2] What a sad testimony to a group of people that have been sent out by God. Most who call themselves "Christians" don't carry out the commission to go. Many do not live sent!

Ray Comfort wisely said, "A church that is waiting for sinners to visit their building is like the police waiting for criminals to visit their station."[3] Our God is a sending God. He sent His best into the world to save us. Jesus is referred to as "sent" forty-four times in the New Testament. The following is just one example.

Mark 9:37
"Whoever welcomes one of these little children in My name welcomes Me; and whoever welcomes Me does not welcome Me but the one who sent Me."

The resurrected Savior shared a resurrection reality! He told His disciples, "The same way the Father sent Me is the same way I am sending you."

John 20:21
Again Jesus said, "Peace be with you! As the Father has sent Me, I am sending you."

Pastor JD Greear once said, "The question is no longer if we are called, only where and how. The call to follow Him is the call to be sent and to send."[4] This message is all over Scripture.

Acts 14 provides a solid connection between decisions for Jesus becoming disciples of Jesus. Paul had just been stoned and left for dead. The very next day, He and Barnabas leave for another town to continue preaching Jesus. Discipleship is costly. Notice what the Bible teaches about discipleship on the heels of Paul's stoning.

Acts 14:21-22
[21] They preached the gospel in that city and won a large number of disciples. Then they returned to Lystra, Iconium and Antioch, [22] strengthening the disciples and encouraging them to remain true to the faith. "We must go through many hardships to enter the kingdom of God," they said. [23] Paul

and Barnabas appointed elders for them in each church and, with prayer and fasting, committed them to the Lord, in whom they had put their trust. ²⁴ *After going through Pisidia, they came into Pamphylia,* ²⁵ *and when they had preached the word in Perga, they went down to Attalia.*

Paul and Barnabas won disciples, strengthened disciples, and they went everywhere they could to preach Jesus and win more disciples. Each place they went, Paul appointed church leaders to assist these new converts in their spiritual growth. It wasn't enough to win a disciple to Christ. Disciples make disciples. They were saved, grew into sold-out believers, and then were sent to reach others for Jesus Christ.

Jesus was the first church planter. Just think how He could have planted the church. Jesus could have brought with Him angels from Heaven such as Michael and Gabriel and had their help in starting the church. Imagine how many souls would have been saved with a church full of angels declaring the message and Jesus at the pulpit! But that's not how Jesus chose to plant His church. Instead of getting heavenly messengers to come down, He converted some earthly men and sent them out as messengers. He assembled a rag-tag group of twelve earthly men and discipled them. Then He told them to go and make disciples of all nations. And then He gave every believer that same commission to make disciples.

God's plan for His church has always been to save, disciple, and send. In fact, Jesus called His first disciples, "apostles."

Luke 6:13
When morning came, He called His disciples to Him and chose twelve of them, whom He also designated apostles:

In Mark 6, Jesus sent out the twelve disciples in pairs and gave them authority over impure spirits. The disciples were sent out and they preached repentance. Notice the term used to describe the twelve disciples when they returned from being sent out.

Mark 6:30

The apostles gathered around Jesus and reported to Him all they had done and taught.

The term "apostles" means "sent out ones." Jesus took disciples, "learners," and turned them into apostles, "ones being sent out." God desires for all of His disciples to be sold out for Him and sent out by Him.

What would happen if His church universally committed themselves to making disciples locally? What if the main agenda for every local church was God's foremost mission for His global church: to make disciples?

Some years ago, a magazine carried a series of pictures that graphically portrayed a horrific story. The first picture was of a large wheat field in western Kansas. The second picture showed a distressed mother standing on the front porch of a farmhouse in the center of that huge wheat field. The accompanying story explained that, when she was not looking, her four-year-old son had wandered away from the house and got lost in the wheat field. The mother and father had frantically looked all day, but the little boy was too short to be seen over the wheat. The third picture showed dozens of friends and neighbors who had heard of the situation and had joined hands the next morning to make a long human chain as they walked through the field searching for the boy. The final devastating picture was of the heartbroken father holding his lifeless son who had been found too late and had died of exposure. The caption underneath the last picture read, "O God, O God, if only we had joined hands sooner!"[5]

It is time for the members of Christ to unite around the mission of our Lord! The church today seems to be arguing over minor issues while ignoring the mandate from our King! And King Jesus is coming back. The Good News of Jesus can't be late! And we want to be found faithful when He comes. May we never forget that we are to be going Christians for a coming Christ.

Chapter 10

Discipleship - The Disciple's Path

In this chapter, we will look at discipleship as it relates to each believer becoming a disciple. In order to make disciples who in turn make other disciples, we have to have a path towards discipleship.

There is a small section of Scripture in Acts 2 that does not fall under worship, evangelism, fellowship, or ministry. When you take all those sections out, here is what remains.

Acts 2:42
They devoted themselves to the apostles teaching . . . and to prayer.

These two offensive weapons for the believer are also the two main tools that lead to discipleship. In our diagram entitled "A Discipleship Revolution", Bible study and prayer connect to every area of discipleship. The intentional process of discipleship will require a commitment to God's Word and prayer for any daily development towards discipleship to occur. One cannot be a disciple of God without being biblical. You will never be a committed follower of Jesus Christ without spending devoted time in prayer with your heavenly Father. These two spiritual disciplines are essential for discipleship.

The first church devoted themselves to the apostles teaching and to prayer. What is intriguing to me is that none of the early Christians were carrying a Bible around in their favorite translation. They didn't have copies of Scripture, but they devoted themselves to the preaching and teaching of God's Word. The apostles, the sent-out-ones, would go to the Temple daily to hear the reading of Scripture. They would most likely have to memorize the teaching and then go repeat it to the early Christians. It was much harder for them to study God's Word in their context, yet they devoted themselves to it. Most Christians today have multiple copies of Scripture at their disposal, not to mention study Bibles, Bible apps, Christian websites, and thousands of free preaching videos at their disposal. We have everything we need to study God's Word. We just don't have the early church's devotion. What we need is a dedication to discipleship that includes a strong commitment to study His Word.

Jesus stresses the importance of the Word of God in the life of a disciple and John's Gospel records it.

John 8:31-32

[31] To the Jews who had believed Him, Jesus said, "If you hold to My teaching, you are really My disciples. [32] Then you will know the truth, and the truth will set you free."

The New King James Version translates John 8:31 as follows: "If you abide in My word, you are My disciples indeed." The word for "hold" or "abide", depending on your translation, is the Greek word "**meno**." It is a word that means, "to continue in, to remain in, to abide."

A believer who has made a decision reads the Word of God. A disciple feeds on the Word of God. God did not give us His Word for information; Christ gave us Scripture for transformation. God did not give us His Word so we could fall in love with the Bible. He gave us His Word so we could fall in love with Him. If you continue in His Word and live it out, you will become a disciple of Jesus Christ. A disciple of Jesus Christ is a doer of God's Word. We obey God's Word because we love the Author who wrote it!

In addition to a devotion to His Word, we need a daily dedicated prayer life. There is not a moment that goes by that we don't have access to speak and listen to the God of all creation. Our Almighty God desires a relationship with His children. How would you feel if your children never spoke with you, unless they needed something from you? I often wonder how our Father feels when, after sending His only Son to die for our sins, so many people don't love Him enough to speak with Him on a regular basis! If you love somebody, you want to spend time with them. It is just a natural byproduct of being passionate about someone. What we need for a more committed prayer life is a renewed passion for our Lord and Savior!

While you cannot program discipleship, you can daily develop into a disciple. A commitment to prayer and the study of God's Word will be the primary way you mature as His disciple.

This pathway to discipleship isn't easy. You will never accidently become a disciple. Discipleship will only occur through intense intentionality and a devotion birthed out of your desire for a relationship with Jesus. It will cost you to become a disciple. That is the difference between those that crowd into Christian concerts and worship services and those that are committed to becoming disciples. In fact, when Jesus got around the masses, He often spoke about the message of discipleship. When Jesus was followed by crowds, He didn't preach church-growth messages. Rather He spoke about the cost of discipleship. Take for example, Luke 14.

Luke 14:25-35

²⁵ Large crowds were traveling with Jesus, and turning to them He said: ²⁶ "If anyone comes to Me and does not hate father and mother, wife and children, brothers and sisters—yes, even their own life—such a person cannot be My disciple. ²⁷ And whoever does not carry their cross and follow Me cannot be My disciple.

²⁸ "Suppose one of you wants to build a tower. Won't you first sit down and estimate the cost to see if you have enough money to complete it? ²⁹ For if you lay the foundation and are not able to finish it, everyone who sees it will ridicule you, ³⁰ saying, 'This person began to build and wasn't able to finish.' ³¹ "Or suppose a king is about to go to war against another king. Won't he first sit down and consider whether he is able with ten thousand men to oppose the one coming against him with twenty thousand? ³² If he is not able, he will send a delegation while the other is still a long way off and will ask for terms of peace. ³³ In the same way, those of you who do not give up everything you have cannot be My disciples. ³⁴ "Salt is good, but if it loses its saltiness, how can it be made salty again? ³⁵ It is fit neither for the soil nor for the manure pile; it is thrown out. "Whoever has ears to hear, let them hear."

Verse 25 states that large crowds were following Jesus. The miracles of Jesus attracted the masses. But Jesus didn't use the power of His miracles to provide Him a platform to preach an easy pathway to becoming His disciple. He wasn't interested in a crowd of false-converts; He was seeking faithful followers. He didn't preach a health-wealth gospel because the pathway to discipleship is full of sacrifice and surrender.

Jesus is always seeking to move people from crowds of spectators towards committed servants. Notice the qualifications for true discipleship that Christ preaches to this crowd of sign-seekers.

(Please note: These six profound statements from Luke 14 come from Allen Parr's YouTube video "Are you a Disciple or Just a Christian?"[1] Allen Parr is a gifted Bible teacher and speaker. His website is allenparr.com. These five truths were used with permission.)

The first qualification Jesus gives is: "**A True Disciple elevates Faith over Family**."

Luke 14:26
[26] *"If anyone comes to Me and does not hate father and mother, wife and children, brothers and sisters—yes, even their own life—such a person cannot be My disciple.*

Jesus is not advocating here that you should hate your earthly family. He is stating that a disciple's love for Him surpasses all other relationships so that all other relationships seem like hate in comparison. In a world full of people that try to fit Jesus into their busy schedule, Jesus states that true disciples prioritize their relationship with Him over everything else.

The second qualification is: "**A True Disciple models Sacrifice over Self-Centeredness**."

Luke 14:26 (Emphasis added by author.)

"If anyone comes to Me and does not hate father and mother, wife and children, brothers and sisters—yes, even their own life—such a person cannot be My disciple.

Jesus stated that you cannot be His disciples unless you hate your own life! Jesus wants you to be willing to sacrifice temporary things for eternal ones. Sacrifice is required over self-centeredness. You cannot be selfish and be His disciples. Selfish people will look out for what is best for themselves. True disciples sacrifice for what is best for the glory of Jesus Christ. Jesus emphasizes this thought at the end of verse 33.

Luke 14:33

. . . those of you who do not give up everything you have cannot be My disciples.

Jesus did not say, "If you don't hate your life, you won't be My disciple." Neither did He suggest, "If you do not give up everything, you might not make it to discipleship." He clearly said, "You cannot be My disciple." We will never be a disciple for Jesus if we are not willing to sacrifice and unselfishly devote ourselves to following Christ.

A third qualification for discipleship is: **"A True Disciple is willing to accept Pain rather than always expecting Pleasure."**

Luke 14:27 (Emphasis added by author.)

*And whoever **does not carry their cross** and follow Me cannot be My disciple.*

The cross of Jesus Christ is not a fashion statement. Rather, it is a death form. Unless we are willing to die to ourselves, we will never live for Jesus. You cannot experience the reality of resurrection power without daily dying-to-self. Carrying a cross has never represented comfort or complacency. The cross of Jesus Christ signifies pain. In fact, our English word "Excruciating" comes from a Latin phrase meaning "Out of the cross." This word came from the cross event because no other existing word could adequately describe the pain associated with crucifixion.

A fourth qualification for following Jesus is: "**A True Disciple elevates Relationship over Religion**."

Luke 14:27 (Emphasis added by author)
*And whoever does not carry their cross **and follow Me** cannot be My disciple.*

A religious person follows rituals and rules. A disciple follows Jesus in an intimate relationship. A true disciple is a Christ-follower. We cannot be His disciple without following Him!

A fifth qualification given by Jesus is: "**A True Disciple values Commitment over Convenience**."

Luke 14:28-33
[28] *"Suppose one of you wants to build a tower. Won't you first sit down and estimate the cost to see if you have enough money to complete it?* [29] *For if you lay the foundation and are not able to finish it, everyone who sees it will ridicule you,* [30] *saying, 'This person began to build and wasn't able to finish.'*
[31] *"Or suppose a king is about to go to war against another king. Won't he first sit down and consider whether he is able with ten thousand men to oppose the one coming against him with twenty thousand?* [32] *If he is not able, he will send a delegation while the other is still a long way off and will ask*

for terms of peace. [33] In the same way, those of you who do not give up everything you have cannot be My disciples.

Both of these biblical examples describe people who couldn't finish the task because they didn't count the cost. It cost to follow Jesus. Discipleship is not convenient. It is not easy dedicating your life to Jesus. It will require an intense commitment and a daily devotion.

A final qualification for discipleship is: "**A True Disciple is Useful to God rather than Useless.**"

Luke 14:34-35
[34] "Salt is good, but if it loses its saltiness, how can it be made salty again? [35] It is fit neither for the soil nor for the manure pile; it is thrown out. "Whoever has ears to hear, let them hear."

In biblical times, salt was used to preserve things. In the hot climate of the Middle East, food would spoil quickly. Salt was a precious commodity because it prevented valuable food from being spoiled. However, salt could lose it saltiness. If salt endured enough heat over time, a chemical reaction would occur that would result in salt losing its flavor. When salt lost its saltiness, it was no longer useful for its intended purposes. Salt was also useful for other reasons. Manure was a common fertilizer in the Middle East. Salt would be thrown on manure piles to prevent the growth of weeds. However, if salt lost its saltiness, it was no longer good for killing weeds. The point of Jesus' salt illustration is that a true disciple of Jesus Christ is useful for His kingdom work. Could Jesus be stressing the fact that many people in the crowds around Him aren't useful for His kingdom? Only the committed followers of Jesus fulfill their purpose in life.

Matthew records this same statement from Jesus in the Sermon on the Mount.

Matthew 5:13
"You are the salt of the earth. But if the salt loses its saltiness, how can it be made salty again? It is no longer good for anything, except to be thrown out and trampled underfoot."

Jesus is teaching the crowds that were following Him this truth: Those who want to be His disciples must understand the sacrifice required and the cost of true commitment. True disciples sacrifice worldly pleasures for spiritual disciplines. The most often stated reason people give for not spending daily time in God's Word and prayer is that they are too busy. The reason most people are too busy is because they have chosen to prioritize worldly things over their devotion to Jesus.

People always make time for what is most important to them. We need a revival and renewal of our love-relationship with Jesus Christ. In order for true biblical discipleship to take place, we need to prioritize our relationship with the Lord. Our dedication to Him will determine our level of discipleship.

Chapter 11

Fellowship - The Disciple's Partnership

Discipleship depends heavily on biblical fellowship. Authentic fellowship provides the relational basis for life-on-life discipleship. Notice the references to fellowship in the description of the early Church.

Acts 2:42, 44, 46
⁴². . . and to fellowship, to the breaking of bread . . .
⁴⁴ All the believers were together and had everything in common. ⁴⁶Every day they continued to meet together in the temple courts. They broke bread in their homes and ate together with glad and sincere hearts.

Scripture describes the early church's dedication as a steadfast commitment from which they derived extraordinary strength. The word "fellowship" is "***koinonia***." It is a beautiful New Testament word that describes a shared participation and a common partnership. It has been defined as a shared life. Our text in Acts 2:42 records its first occurrence in the New Testament.

There is a growing social isolation in our world today. Many people sit behind computer screens and cell phones for most of their communication. They live in gated communities and can even shop online for groceries. Today, people live in seclusion and have everything delivered to their front door. There is a growing epidemic of loneliness in our society. Yet, we were all created for community.

First of all, we have a Creator who Himself lives in community. He is "**The God of Fellowship**." The Bible teaches that God exists eternally in community. It is the mystery of the Trinity. While the Trinity is difficult to fully explain, one thing is for certain – one God exists in three persons: God the Father, God the Son, and God the Holy Spirit. A study of the Word reveals the Trinity at work in creation.

Genesis 1:1-3
¹ In the beginning God created the heavens and the earth.
² Now the earth was formless and empty, darkness was over the surface of the deep, and the Spirit of God was hovering over the waters.³ And God said, "Let there be light," and there was light.

I know what you are thinking after studying the Scripture above. You notice God the Father, and God the Spirit, but where is God the Son? He is in verse 3. The clue is in the words, "God said," and John 1 finishes the rest of the puzzle.

John 1:1-5, 14
¹ In the beginning was the Word, and the Word was with God, and the Word was God. ² He was with God in the beginning. ³ Through Him all things were made; without Him nothing was made that has been made. ⁴ In Him was life, and that life was the light of all mankind. ⁵ The light shines in the darkness, and the darkness has not overcome it. . . . ¹⁴ The Word

became flesh and made His dwelling among us. We have seen His glory, the glory of the one and only Son, who came from the Father, full of grace and truth.

The Word is Jesus. The God who spoke creation into existence is Jesus. Colossians reveals that the world came into being through Jesus Christ, the Son of God.

Colossians 1:15-17

15 The Son is the image of the invisible God, the firstborn over all creation. 16 For in Him all things were created: things in heaven and on earth, visible and invisible, whether thrones or powers or rulers or authorities; all things have been created through Him and for Him. 17 He is before all things, and in Him all things hold together.

Therefore, from the beginning of creation, we learn that God exists in community. He is the God of fellowship because He lives in community.

God created us in His own image. He created us in the image of community and therefore, we have a longing built in us for fellowship. Notice the Trinity referenced in the pronouns found in the following Scripture.

Genesis 1:26-27

26 Then God said, "Let Us make mankind in Our image, in Our likeness, so that they may rule over the fish in the sea and the birds in the sky, over the livestock and all the wild animals, and over all the creatures that move along the ground." 27 So God created mankind in His own image, in the image of God He created them; male and female He created them.

After Genesis 1 and 2 comes The Fall in Genesis 3. While we were created for community, that fellowship was lost because of sin. Sin separated us from the communal relationship that God had originally created. However, God is the restorer of everything that is broken. Father, Son, and Holy Spirit are dedicated to restoring us back into the community in which we were originally created to enjoy.

Secondly, notice, "**The Goal of Fellowship**." Our God of fellowship has a goal for fellowship. God desires that His children have the same fellowship as the Trinity shares. That is what Jesus expresses in John 17.

John 17:11
I will remain in the world no longer, but they are still in the world, and I am coming to You. Holy Father, protect them by the power of Your name, the name You gave Me, so that they may be one as We are one.

Jesus desires that His followers have the same intimate fellowship with the Father that He Himself has with God. God wants to restore the community that sin has separated us from. You can see this restitution discussed in God's Word.

Ephesians 2:17-22
[17] He came and preached peace to you who were far away and peace to those who were near. [18] For through Him we both have access to the Father by one Spirit. [19] Consequently, you are no longer foreigners and strangers, but fellow citizens with God's people and also members of His household, [20] built on the foundation of the apostles and prophets, with Christ Jesus Himself as the chief cornerstone. [21] In Him the whole building is joined together and rises to

become a holy temple in the Lord. ²² And in Him you too are being built together to become a dwelling in which God lives by His Spirit.

We belong in a family for fellowship. And please don't confuse fellowship with just hanging out with people and eating. Many churches think that if they shook hands and ate dinner on the grounds, that fellowship took place. No, the biblical meaning of fellowship is much deeper than just hanging out together. That is because being a Christian is not just believing, it is belonging. We need each other and we were created for true fellowship.

Ecclesiastes 4:9-12
⁹ Two are better than one, because they have a good return for their labor: ¹⁰ If either of them falls down, one can help the other up. But pity anyone who falls and has no one to help them up. ¹¹ Also, if two lie down together, they will keep warm. But how can one keep warm alone? ¹² Though one may be overpowered, two can defend themselves. A cord of three strands is not quickly broken.

Closeness of community occurs as we love each other with the love of Christ and forgive one another because, in Christ, God has forgiven us. True biblical fellowship develops us as disciples as we worship God together and as we take Communion together. This closeness exists as we are real and authentic with each other in a family of faith!

One way to see this biblical community is to study the "one another" passages in Scripture. These verses give us an overview of a true community of believers. Here are just a few:

- Love one another. (John 13:34, 15:12)
- Live in harmony with one another. (Romans 12:16)
- Serve one another. (John 13:1-20; Galatians 5:13)
- Submit to one another. (Ephesians 5:21)
- Encourage one another. (1 Thessalonians 5:11)

Christians need one another because we were created for community by a God who exists in a trinitarian relationship. It is through this genuine fellowship with God and an authentic fellowship with other believers, that we continue to mature as disciples of Jesus Christ.

Jesus loved the first disciples. He spent quantity and quality time with His men in order to make them His disciples. Quality time occurs in the midst of quantity time. The more time you spend together with Jesus, the more you will hear His voice. The better you know God, the greater your opportunity will be to grow in Christlikeness. Relationships grow in direct proportion to meaningful time spent together.

The same is true for the fellowship of believers through discipleship. The more you are mentored by a seasoned saint, the more you model that mentor's Christlikeness. You become like-minded and one in spirit because of the time you spend together.

This need for biblical fellowship can be seen in the terminology used to describe Christ-followers in Scripture. In Matthew 4, Jesus calls His first disciples to be His followers. In Matthew 10, Jesus called His disciples, "Apostles," which means "Sent ones." In John 15, Jesus called these disciples, "His friends." Jesus wants us to follow Him so that we can be sent out for His glory and grow in our fellowship with Him. He wants us to follow Him to the friendship stage of our relationship. Notice the context of Jesus declaring that His disciples are friends.

John 15:12-17

12 My command is this: Love each other as I have loved you. 13 Greater love has no one than this: to lay down one's life for one's friends. 14 You are My friends if you do what I command. 15 I no longer call you servants, because a servant does not know his master's business. Instead, I have called you friends, for everything that I learned from My Father I have made known to you. 16 You did not choose Me, but I chose you and appointed you so that you might go and bear fruit—fruit that will last—and so that whatever you ask in My name the Father will give you.17 This is My command: Love each other.

Jesus commanded His first disciples to love one another with the same love He had modeled to them. He told them that the proof of their friendship stemmed from their obedience to His commands. As they matured as disciples, they moved from His servants to His friends. Part of the fruit of discipleship is the fellowship with the Father that leads to friendship. Therefore, Jesus closes this section of Scripture the same way He started it: with a command for His disciples to love one another. Love forges the believers into a fellowship that produces genuine friends. And biblical fellowship develops believers into disciples that produce much fruit!

Chapter 12

Ministry - The Disciple's Posture

Discipleship leads to ministry and serving Jesus builds disciples. You are never more like Jesus than when you are serving. The early church demonstrated sacrificial ministry.

Acts 2:45
They sold their property and possessions to give to anyone who had a need.

The early believers sacrificed for the benefit of others. A mark of a true disciple of Jesus Christ is selfless service. Their love for Jesus and for one another was the motive behind their ministry. Neither the early church nor Jesus broadcasted their ministries; they simply ministered to people. The world will remember our influence more by our actions than by our words.

The two main New Testament words for ministry are "***diakoneo***" and "***douleuo***" The first term means "to serve" and the second translates "to serve as a slave." The biblical concept of ministry was always connected to service. Therefore, a true disciple of Jesus Christ takes on the posture of a servant.

Another Greek word used for "minister" is "*hyperetes*" which literally translates as "the under-rower." This is the word for servant found in 1 Corinthians 4:1-2.

1 Corinthians 4:1-2
¹ This, then, is how you ought to regard us: as servants of Christ and as those entrusted with the mysteries God has revealed. ² Now it is required that those who have been given a trust must prove faithful.

This New Testament word for servant describes the rower in the bottom of the ship. The rower is working hard but nobody knows that he is down there in the lowest section of the boat. Several lessons are gleaned from this word picture. All the servants had to row together in obscurity so the captain could get to his destination. They worked and labored so that the captain could be honored and recognized. This is a great picture of the Christian as a servant of Christ ministering so that God gets the glory He deserves.

God has called us to serve Him! It is a privilege and the real motive for any ministry. Jesus modeled servanthood to His disciples over and over again. And then He called them to serve the same way He had demonstrated to them. Some believers serve God out of duty and not delight.

Most Christians are aware that we should love God with all of our hearts. However, did you know you are to serve Him that way also? Notice the following Scripture:

Deuteronomy 11:13
So if you faithfully obey the commands I am giving you today—to love the Lord your God and to serve Him with all your heart and with all your soul—

You could say that loving God goes hand-in-hand with serving Him! All throughout Scripture, we read of those who served God. God's ministry to His children was accomplished through His servants.

Let's take a look at the topic of servants in Scripture under three headings.

1. Servants throughout Scripture
Tucked away ever so subtlety is this picture of serving in Scripture. We know that many of the Old Testament saints served the Lord. For example, Noah served the Lord by obediently building an ark before anyone had ever seen rain. Have you noticed how many Old Testament heroes are called servants?

Abraham was called God's servant.

Psalm 105:42
For He remembered His holy promise given to His servant Abraham.

Moses was referred to as God's servant.

Deuteronomy 34:5
And Moses the servant of the Lord died there in Moab, as the Lord had said.

The Lord called David, "My servant."

2 Samuel 7:8
Now then, tell My servant David, 'This is what the Lord Almighty says: I took you from the pasture, from tending the flock, and appointed you ruler over My people Israel.'

All of these aforementioned servants were important, but even their great service couldn't restore lost humanity back into a right relationship with God. These servants of God foreshadowed the only Servant who could bring redemption.

2. Our Savior as The Servant

Isaiah prophesied about "The Suffering Servant" in what are known as "Servant Songs" in Isaiah chapters 42, 49, 50, and 52-53. The following is a brief example of these songs.

Isaiah 52:13-14

[13] See, My Servant will act wisely; He will be raised and lifted up and highly exalted. [14] Just as there were many who were appalled at Him — His appearance was so disfigured beyond that of any human being and His form marred beyond human likeness—

Isaiah 53:5-7

[5]But He was pierced for our transgressions, He was crushed for our iniquities; the punishment that brought us peace was on Him, and by His wounds we are healed. [6] We all, like sheep, have gone astray, each of us has turned to our own way; and the Lord has laid on Him the iniquity of us all. [7] He was oppressed and afflicted, yet He did not open His mouth; He was led like a lamb to the slaughter, and as a sheep before its shearers is silent, so He did not open His mouth.

These "Servant Songs" point to the One True Faithful Servant who fully atoned for the sins of mankind. The religious leaders didn't take Jesus' life from Him. Jesus willingly laid His life down as a Servant! He modeled it through washing the disciple's feet and taught it through parables. He is the Servant! He was obedient to death, even death on a cross. Jesus is not only King of kings and Lord of lords; He is also the Servant above all other servants.

One of the many things I love about Jesus is that everything He calls us to, He already exemplified in His life, death, and resurrection.

3. The Significance of Servanthood

Servanthood is so important to Jesus that when He gave His four purpose statements, one in each of the Gospels, two of them directly deal with being a servant. In addition, the remaining two purpose statements were made possible because Jesus served!

Matthew 20:28
". . . just as the Son of Man did not come to be served, but to serve, and to give His life as a ransom for many."

Mark 10:45
"For even the Son of Man did not come to be served, but to serve, and to give His life as a ransom for many."

Luke 19:10
"For the Son of Man came to seek and to save the lost."

John 10:10
"The thief comes only to steal and kill and destroy; I have come that they may have life, and have it to the full."

The Old Testament servants all pointed to The Suffering Servant – our Savior. And our Savior calls us to live a life of service.

This concludes our chapters on the Discipleship Revolution. We have covered briefly how worship, evangelism, fellowship, and ministry connect to discipleship. This study has also discussed how the study of God's Word and prayer connect to each of these areas of spiritual discipline. The result of devotion to a biblical approach to these areas bathed in prayer leads to discipleship. Remember however, "**Practice makes progress; Jesus makes perfect**." God has called us to make disciples, mature disciples, and multiply disciples. Worship, evangelism, fellowship, and ministry are four of the best paths to discipleship while also being byproducts of discipleship. Discipleship is the hinge that connects the framework of God's Word to the fullness of all that God has for you. Daily walk through the door of discipleship that God places before you. Obeying "**God's Divine Demand**" will give you "**The Daily Development**" you desperately need to reach your full potential in Jesus Christ.

In the next chapter, which will conclude this book, we will look at some possible intentional pathways that could lead to discipleship.

Chapter 13

The Daily Development of Discipleship

There is a desperate need in the church today to move people from their decision for Christ to becoming disciples of Christ. We need to move from an aisle we walk down to a path we live out. Many people have walked down an aisle of a church and made a decision. However, many don't move from that decision to a pathway towards discipleship. It is a great privilege to identify with Christ in baptism. It is an enormous responsibility to walk with the Lord on a daily basis. The church needs an intentional process and a clear path to discipleship.

Discipleship takes time. A six-week class does not exist that will produce a fully devoted disciple of Jesus Christ. The movement from followers to friends takes time and consistency. True disciples are sown and grown not instant and inconsistent. Therefore, this daily development will involve a pathway and a process, not a program and a schedule.

The struggle in this daily development of discipleship is creating an approach that is both simple and reproducible. A process of discipleship also needs to make sense in the context of the local church. So, there are multiple strategies for discipleship that could follow the biblical model.

It is this author's opinion that the discipleship process needs to begin with a firm foundation of teachings on the basics of our faith. This first part in the development towards discipleship should include a clear explanation of what is both required for salvation and what results from salvation. The marks of discipleship should also be taught from a biblical perspective. Then, the fourfold purpose of worship, evangelism, fellowship and ministry should be connected to the maturity of discipleship. As this book has discussed, Bible study and prayer are foundational teaching doctrines necessary in this initial journey. While there is much that could fall under the category "The Basics of our Faith," these represent a good starting point. This first section of discipleship could last from several weeks to several months, depending on the approach.

The discipleship process should be done with a qualified mentor in same-sex groups of three to five people for maximum effect. One-on-one discipleship is prone to lead to a counseling session, while larger groups run the risk of a talker dominating the group time. The discipleship approach needs to be on a weekly basis to reap the consistency that true biblical discipleship demands.

There needs to be an intentional strategy so that the discipleship process is not only founded on, but continues in, the study of God's Word and prayer. At some point in the initial phase of doctrinal teaching, tools for the spiritual disciplines of Bible study and prayer need to be introduced. These tools will serve to continue the discipleship process long after the foundations are taught. There are many great resources for these tools already available.

Please use whatever tool works best for you as long as an intentional ongoing process of discipleship is possible. I have developed a tool for each of these spiritual disciplines that I will share over the next several pages. Examples will also be given so that you can better understand the process.

In order to learn how to study God's Word, we will look at an acrostic for **B.I.B.L.E.** that will serve as a pattern for approaching daily time in Scripture.

B stands for **behold**. Behold is a biblical word that means, "to fix your eyes upon, to see with attention, and to observe with care." Another definition for this word is "to perceive through sight or apprehension." It is a great word to remember as you start your study of God's Word. The first thing we do as we study God's Word is to focus on a text in order to comprehend the biblical message. Beholding God through His Word has the power to transform our lives.

2 Corinthians 3:18 (ESV)
18 And we all, with unveiled face, beholding the glory of the Lord, are being transformed into the same image from one degree of glory to another. For this comes from the Lord who is the Spirit.

If we can behold God daily in His word, we can become what God has called us to be. Beholding Him changes us and matures us towards discipleship. As we approach His Word, we should pray along with the psalmist to grasp all that God has for us in Scripture.

Psalm 119:33-37
33 Teach me, Lord, the way of Your decrees, that I may follow it to the end. 34 Give me understanding, so that I may keep Your law and obey it with all my heart. 35 Direct me in the path of Your commands, for there I find delight. 36 Turn my

heart toward Your statutes and not toward selfish gain. *[37] Turn my eyes away from worthless things; preserve my life according to Your word.*

I stands for **invite**. As we study God's Word, we invite the Holy Spirit to give us wisdom to discern the truths of the Bible. We need the Spirit of God to enlighten us as we invite Him through prayer to teach us from the Scriptures. During this time, we pray through the Scripture. We read and ask the Holy Spirit to give us counsel along the way.

John 14:26
[26] But the Advocate, the Holy Spirit, whom the Father will send in My name, will teach you all things and will remind you of everything I have said to you.

The second **B** stands for **believe**. In every study of God's Word, there is a truth to believe and apply to our personal lives. When we study the Bible, we have to accept His Word by faith. Scripture will only be at work in our lives if we trust in the truths that we behold.

1 Thessalonians 2:13
[13] And we also thank God continually because, when you received the word of God, which you heard from us, you accepted it not as a human word, but as it actually is, the word of God, which is indeed at work in you who believe.

The **L** signifies **learn**. We don't read the Bible for information. We study the Bible to learn how to apply Scripture to our lives. The word disciple simply means, "learner." In order to become His disciple, we must learn His Word. The Bible itself declares that all Scripture has a purpose for us to learn. This is where deeper study of God's Word develops disciples.

2 Timothy 3:14-17
[14] But as for you, continue in what you have learned and have become convinced of, because you know those from whom you learned it, [15] and how from infancy you have known the Holy Scriptures, which are able to make you wise for salvation through faith in Christ Jesus. [16] All Scripture is God-breathed and is useful for teaching, rebuking, correcting and training in righteousness, [17] so that the servant of God[may be thoroughly equipped for every good work.

God gave us His Word to teach us how to grow as His disciples. Those who delight in God's Word and learn it will live fruitful lives.

Psalm 1:1-3
[1]Blessed is the one who does not walk in step with the wicked or stand in the way that sinners take or sit in the company of mockers, [2]but whose delight is in the law of the Lord, and who meditates on His law day and night. [3] That person is like a tree planted by streams of water, which yields its fruit in season and whose leaf does not wither—whatever they do prospers.

The **E** refers to **engrave** it on your heart. If you have God's Word written on your heart, it will be applied to your lives. God wants us to be doers of His Word.

Hebrews 10:16
"This is the covenant I will make with them after that time, says the Lord. I will put my laws in their hearts, and I will write them on their minds."

The Greek word for "write" in this verse is "***epigrapho***" and means, "to inscribe, engrave the thoughts, or to write upon." This verse explains that God will engrave His Word on our minds. We need to study God's Word. We must meditate on Scripture until the Word is placed upon our hearts. This doesn't happen by speed-reading through your quiet time. As we meditate on His Word and be still, the Bible permeates our minds and we learn to know God better.

Deuteronomy 11:18
Fix these words of Mine in your hearts and minds; tie them as symbols on your hands and bind them on your foreheads.

We need to study God's Word so intently, that we attain more than biblical knowledge. As the Ten Commandments were engraved on stone tablets, we need God's commands written on our hearts. We need God's Word spiritually etched into our hearts and inscribed in our minds.

Let's take the **B.I.B.L.E.** approach to the study of God's Word and walk through an example together. A study of Romans 12:1-2 will serve as our example.

Romans 12:1-2
¹ Therefore, I urge you, brothers and sisters, in view of God's mercy, to offer your bodies as a living sacrifice, holy and pleasing to God—this is your true and proper worship. ² Do not conform to the pattern of this world, but be transformed

by the renewing of your mind. Then you will be able to test and approve what God's will is—His good, pleasing and perfect will.

Behold "Paul is urging me to enter into proper worship by how I offer my body as a sacrifice to God. The way I live with this vessel that God gave me is my truest form of worship. Don't be conformed to worldly living. Instead be transformed by continually renewing my mind. This is the way to find God's will for my life."

Invite "Holy Spirit, please counsel me as I journey through this Scripture. I do not want just information. Please bring transformation to my life through the strength of Your Word and the power of Your Might. Help me to view Your mercy clearly so that I can offer my body consistently to You. Remind me, Holy Spirit, that the truest worship is what I do with the way I live this life. Help me to allow You to transform me from the inside out. Please don't allow me to conform to this world. Please lead me to Your will because only Your will is good, pleasing, and perfect. Direct my steps through this Scripture, Spirit of the Living God. Give me wisdom to live it out as a doer of Your Word. Amen."

Believe "What truths are in this Scripture that I need to believe and put my trust in? God's mercies motivate my worship. Living pleasing to God is the foundational level of worship. Offering my body as a living sacrifice occurs as I resist the world's influences and live transformed by Christ in me. This way of worship will lead me to God's perfect will for this life He has blessed me to live."

Learn **(For this section, you can study from free resources like biblehub.com and biblegateway.com.)**

"This verse starts with 'Therefore.' When I see this word in Scripture, I ask myself, 'What is it there for?' This word points me back to the doctrinal section of the book of Romans. Like most of Paul's writings, there is a 'what you believe' section followed by a 'how you behave' section. So, everything Paul teaches up to this point in the book of Romans leads me to this moment in Scripture. This is a significant point in Scripture that culminates in some serious truth for my life."

"The word 'urge' is a Greek word *parakaleo*. It means, 'to call alongside to encourage and implore.' Paul is walking alongside of me strongly encouraging me to learn to live this way."

"The word for 'offer' means, 'to present or exhibit.' God wants the way I live to be an exhibit of His mercies. Living in His perfect will is a huge part of worship because it exhibits to the world God's transforming power."

"The word 'proper' is the Greek word '*logikos*.' This is where the English words logic and logical stem from. The Scripture describes the logical way a Christian is to live their life."

"In Greek, the word 'conformed' has the word 'scheme' in it. The world always tries to get me to fall for its schemes. Don't fall for lies this world has to offer."

"The word 'transformed' is '*metamorpho*.' This is where the word 'metamorphosis' originates from. Like a caterpillar is completely transformed into a butterfly, God wants to transform my life into something beautiful for His glory."

"This way of offering myself to God on a daily basis proves that I am living in His will. His will is good and perfect. It is pleasing and fulfilling to live transformed by God."

Engrave "Lord, please write these truths on my heart so that they will mark my life. As I continue to meditate on this word and all I have learned, please drive these principles deep into my mind and my soul. Help me to remember them so that I can daily live this way. Whisper them into my spirit so that I can walk by them. Thank You for the truths You have given me today from Your Holy Word. I seek to be a doer of Your Word. Please let these truths be lived out through my daily life and start today. Thank You Jesus for speaking to me today. Keep guiding me through Your Word. Amen."

In order to go deeper in prayer, I have another tool from the acrostic for **P.R.A.Y.E.R.**

The **P** refers to **praise**. Jesus teaches us in the model prayer in Matthew 6 to begin with praise. Jesus says, "This, then, is how you should pray: 'Our Father in heaven, hallowed be Your name, . . .'" Beginning your prayer with praise starts your focus on the greatness of God rather than on the circumstances of life. The Bible has much to say about praise.

Isaiah 25:1

¹ Lord, you are My God; I will exalt You and praise Your name, for in perfect faithfulness You have done wonderful things, things planned long ago.

Psalm 103:1-5

¹ Praise the Lord, my soul; all my inmost being, praise His holy name. ² Praise the Lord, my soul, and forget not all His benefits— ³ who forgives all your sins and heals all your diseases, ⁴ who redeems your life from the pit and crowns you with love and compassion, ⁵ who satisfies your desires with good things so that your youth is renewed like the eagle's.

Psalm 63:3-4

³ Because Your love is better than life, my lips will glorify You. ⁴ I will praise You as long as I live, and in Your name I will lift up my hands.

The **R** stands for **repent**. After I praise God, I confess any sin in my life. I then turn from that sin and turn back to God in repentance. Daily repentance keeps sin from setting up patterns in my heart. The way to holiness is a daily pursuit. Any sin left unchecked in the life of a believer can reap havoc in a believer's life. The biblical word for repentance means "a change of mind that leads to a change of direction." I cannot allow my mind to rationalize sin. I must daily call sin what it is: Defiant disobedience in the face of God. If my mind has started to excuse sinful behavior or attitudes, I need to change that mindset immediately and turn back to God in repentance.

2 Chronicles 7:14
if My people, who are called by My name, will humble them-selves and pray and seek My face and turn from their wicked ways, then I will hear from heaven, and I will forgive their sin and will heal their land.

Acts 3:19
Repent, then, and turn to God, so that your sins may be wiped out, that times of refreshing may come from the Lord,

2 Timothy 2:19
[19] Nevertheless, God's solid foundation stands firm, sealed with this inscription: "The Lord knows those who are His," and, "Everyone who confesses the name of the Lord must turn away from wickedness."

The **A** denotes **asking**. The Bible says in James 4 that we do not have because we do not ask, or we ask with the wrong motives. Prayer is a time to ask for God's power in your life. It is also a time to intercede on behalf of others. God is never too busy for your questions. Ask Him all your questions because He has all the answers!

Matthew 7:7-8
[7] "Ask and it will be given to you; seek and you will find; knock and the door will be opened to you. [8] For everyone who asks receives; the one who seeks finds; and to the one who knocks, the door will be opened."

1 John 5:14-15
[14] This is the confidence we have in approaching God: that if we ask anything according to His will, He hears us. [15] And if we know that He hears us—whatever we ask—we know that we have what we asked of Him.

James 1:5
[5] If any of you lacks wisdom, you should ask God, who gives generously to all without finding fault, and it will be given to you.

The **Y** stands for **yield**. Yielding to God means surrendering your will to His on a regular basis. Just as a yield sign on a roadway symbolizes yielding the right-away, spiritually I need to daily surrender my rights to His rule in my life. A life of daily surrender leads to the development of a daily dependence on God. Disciples of Jesus Christ follow the leading of their Savior rather than living for themselves.

Romans 6:12-13, 16
[12] Therefore do not let sin reign in your mortal body so that you obey its evil desires. [13] Do not offer any part of yourself to sin as an instrument of wickedness, but rather offer yourselves to God as those who have been brought from death to life; and offer every part of yourself to Him as an instrument of righteousness. . . [16] Don't you know that when you offer yourselves to someone as obedient slaves, you are slaves of the one you obey—whether you are slaves to sin, which leads to death, or to obedience, which leads to righteousness?

Matthew 6:33
"But seek first His kingdom and His righteousness, and all these things will be given to you as well."

Philippians 2:5-7

⁵ In your relationships with one another, have the same mindset as Christ Jesus: ⁶ Who, being in very nature God, did not consider equality with God something to be used to His own advantage; ⁷ rather, He made Himself nothing by taking the very nature of a servant, being made in human likeness.

The **E** refers to **enjoy**. In your time of daily dialogue with Jesus, enjoy spending time in His presence. Appreciate the experience of your relationship with the God who created everything. Seek to understand His love for you. Be encouraged by His mercies and grace. Don't rush through this time with the Lord. You are in the presence of King Jesus who is Lord of all!

Psalm 46:10

He says, "Be still, and know that I am God; I will be exalted among the nations, I will be exalted in the earth."

Psalm 84:1-2

¹ How lovely is Your dwelling place, Lord Almighty! ² My soul yearns, even faints, for the courts of the Lord; my heart and my flesh cry out for the living God.

Psalm 16:11

You make known to me the path of life; You will fill me with joy in Your presence, with eternal pleasures at Your right hand.

The second **R** stands for **renew**. Allow this time with Father God to renew your spirit. End each time of prayer with a restored joy in who you are in Jesus. As you spend time daily in His presence, your soul is reinvigorated, and your spirit is replenished. This intimate time with your Savior will give you strength to develop daily into the disciple that He has called you to become.

Psalm 27:8

My heart says of You, "Seek His face!" Your face, Lord, I will seek.

Psalm 51:10

Create in me a pure heart, O God, and renew a steadfast spirit within me.

Philippians 4:8-9, 13

[8] Finally, brothers and sisters, whatever is true, whatever is noble, whatever is right, whatever is pure, whatever is lovely, whatever is admirable—if anything is excellent or praiseworthy—think about such things. [9] Whatever you have learned or received or heard from me, or seen in me—put it into practice. And the God of peace will be with you. . . [13] I can do all this through Him who gives me strength.

Let's take the **P.R.A.Y.E.R.** approach and walk through an example together.

"Father God, I **praise** You for who You are and for all You have done! You are my rock and my redeemer. You are the peace that passes all understanding. I praise You for Your forgiveness and grace. Thank You for saving my soul! I love You with my whole heart. You alone are worthy of praise! Jesus thank You for leaving Your throne room in glory and making the way of salvation available to whosoever will trust in Your name.

I confess that I did not seek You throughout the day yesterday. I confess that my attitude has been angry, and I have been short with the family You blessed me with. I am truly sorry Lord, and I repent of my sin. I admit that my mind tends to be overly critical and I get negative in my thoughts. I **repent** of these sins and turn back to You and the joy You bring. Guide me in a continued path of holiness. Guard my thoughts Lord and help me to honor You in my attitude.

God, I **ask** that You help me to be the man of God that I need to be. Help me to be the Christian husband, father, and leader that would bring glory to Your name. I desperately need You to bring restoration to my family and hope to my home. God please heal the brokenhearted that are grieving loss today. I beg You Lord to bring healing to our land. I ask that You bring revival to this country by bringing revival to the heart of every Christian. Unite us Lord around Your purpose for Your church.

In this moment Lord, I **yield** to Your will in my life. I surrender to Your lordship in this life You have given me. I submit to Your leadership in my life. I come before You as Your servant Lord. Speak Lord, for Your servant is listening. Help me to hear Your truth so that I can follow Your will. Guide me in the paths of righteousness for Your namesake.

I long to be in Your presence. I **enjoy** this time with You. It is a privilege to be Your child. I love having You as my Heavenly Father. Thank You for the joy of my salvation that only You can bring. Thank You for the privilege of being in Your presence. I find complete peace through my time with You. I love You Lord!

Renew me today, Lord. Reinvigorate my soul to live this day for You and You alone. Restore me Lord back into a right relationship with You. I find strength in serving You. I can accomplish everything today that You have called me to do, because I know You will enable and empower me. Keep my mind renewed. As I go about this day, help me to continue to have this conversation with You. I need You every second of this day. Help me to pray without ceasing! I pray all this in My Savior's name, the precious name of Jesus. So be it! Amen."

If we could spend time daily dialoguing with God through prayer and learning His Word, God can empower us to become disciples for His glory. God would never call us to something that He will not also equip us to become! He desires for disciples who make disciples, and He will grant His power to those devoted to His will. Let's move from decisions to disciples. May we become all that God desires us to be. Let us not stop short or settle for less. God can lead forgiven people to follow Him to fruitful lives.

In the Appendix of this book, I have included blank forms for journaling through the spiritual disciplines of **B.I.B.L.E.** and **P.R.A.Y.E.R.** I also hope in the future to make a journal available with these acrostics so that you can have one place to keep everything God is revealing to you.

These tools will teach you to feed yourselves from the Word of God and prayer. These two main offensive weapons in spiritual warfare will help you to be battle-ready as you face each new day in your discipleship journey. Learning daily from His Word and dialoging daily with Your Lord will lead you to follow Him closely. Follow your Master and Mentor Jesus Christ as He leads you to daily discipleship.

As you mature as disciples, and meet regularly in your discipleship groups, these two tools will become valuable resources to help you lead fruitful lives for Jesus. During your weekly meetings, you should share one of you **B.I.B.L.E.** journals with the group. You will have seven to choose from each week. By sharing what God is teaching you through His Word, others in the group will benefit from the insight the

Holy Spirit gave you. And you will spiritually profit from what each person in your discipleship group shares when it is their turn.

I hope and pray that God has challenged and encouraged you in discipleship. One day, we will all give an account of our lives before the Lord. He will hold us accountable to what He commanded us to do. I hope we all hear Him say, "Well done." In the meantime, I trust that God will give you great joy as you live out His purpose. Becoming a disciple of Jesus Christ and making disciples for Him brings the greatest satisfaction in life. May God bless you in your journey.

Ray Cummings

Appendix A
"B.I.B.L.E."

B **Behold** 2 Corinthians 3:18 / Psalm 119:33-37

_____

_____

_____

I **Invite** John 14:26

_____

_____

_____

B **Believe** 1 Thessalonians 2:13

_____

_____

_____

L **Learn** 2 Timothy 3:14-16/Psalm 1:1-3

_____

_____

_____

E **Engrave** Hebrews 10:16/Deuteronomy 11:18

_____

_____

_____

Appendix B
"P.R.A.Y.E.R."

P   **Praise**   Isaiah 25:1/Psalm 103:1-5/Psalm 63:3-4

_____

_____

R   **Repent**   2 Chronicles 7:14/Acts 3:19/2 Timothy 2:19

_____

_____

A   **Ask**   Matthew 7:7-8/1 John 5:14/James 1:5

_____

_____

Y   **Yield**   Romans 6:12-13, 16/Matthew 6:33/Philippians 2:5-7

_____

_____

E   **Enjoy**   Psalm 46:10/Psalm 84:1-2/Psalm 16:11

_____

_____

R   **Renew**   Psalm 27:8/Psalm 51:10/Philippians 4:8-9, 13

_____

_____

_____

Small Group Study Guide

Chapter 1
The Five-Fold Commission of Christ

Scripture to Discuss
- Matthew 28:18-20
- Mark 16:15
- Luke 24:46-49
- John 20:21
- Acts 1:8

Truths to Consider
- Jesus gave a clear command in His final commission to His disciples.
- Matthew presents the promise.
- Mark states the parameters.
- Luke centers on the preaching.
- John gives us the pattern.
- Acts displays the power.
- The purpose Jesus lived for is now the purpose His disciples live out.

Questions to Reflect
- What is the "Five-Fold Commission of Christ" and why is it essential to your Christian life?
- What is God's purpose for every believer?
- What is the difference between Bible study and discipleship?

Chapter 2
The Divine Demand from the Great Commission

Scripture to Discuss
- Matthew 28:16-20

Truths to Consider
- The Great Commission has been handed down to every follower of Jesus Christ.
- The command to "Make Disciples" is the main imperative of the Great Commission.
- Jesus said, "Out of who I am, go and make disciples" and "I even I will be with you always."

Questions to Reflect
- How does the beginning and end of the Great Commission give you both confidence and courage?
- What are the four commands of the Great Commission?
- Which ones are you obeying? Which ones are you ignoring?
- What does "Double Down on Discipleship" mean?

Chapter 3
Discipleship Defined

Scripture to Discuss
- Romans 10:9-10, 13
- Matthew 4:19-20
- John 15:8
- Romans 7:4
- Matthew 3:8
- Hebrews 10:14
- Hebrews 12:11
- 1 Timothy 4:7-10

Truths to Consider
- Discipleship is the intentional process whereby forgiven people become faithful followers of Jesus Christ who bear much fruit.
- "Practice makes Progress; Jesus makes Perfect." – Dr. Ronnie Kent
- A decision is made in a moment, but a disciple doesn't just happen in the meantime. The path to discipleship takes sacrifice, dedication, and perseverance. Discipleship is an intentional process.

Questions to Reflect
- What are your thoughts on the definition of discipleship given in this chapter?
- Do you have an intentional strategy for discipleship? If so, what is your plan?
- According to this definition, where are you on the process of becoming a disciple?
- What does discipleship mean to you personally?

Chapter 4
The Hinge of Discipleship

Scripture to Discuss
- John 10:7, 9
- Acts 14:27-28
- Psalm 24:7
- Matthew 7:7-8
- Revelation 3:7-8

Truths to Consider
- Jesus is King and He holds the keys to the kingdom. When He opens a door, no one can shut it. And when He closes doors, no one can open them. God has placed before His church an open door that no one can shut.
- Discipleship connects God's Word to His will for your life.
- If we want God to swing open the door of opportunity for His church, we need to get back to a clear focus on discipleship.

Questions to Reflect
- What are your thoughts on "The Hinge of Discipleship"?
- Is Discipleship in your church just a fad or is there an intentional process in place? Explain your answer.
- What can you do to help your church obey God's command to "Make Disciples"?
- What open door has God provided that you need to walk through?

Chapter 5
The Model for Making Disciples

Scripture to Discuss
- Acts 1:7-8
- Acts 2:28
- Acts 2:42-47

Truths to Consider
- Jesus wasn't into building crowds; He was focused on making disciples. And Jesus knows that the only way to make disciples is through meaningful, personal, and intimate relationships.
- Most leaders in today's church can't convince Christians to go to church. These first disciples came to Christ and then committed their lives to the cause!
- Jesus basically moved them in their thinking from worrying about *when*, to focusing on *Who* will be with them each step of the journey. We get so caught up in times and places that we miss His truth and the power of the Holy Spirit that's all around us.
- We will never have more peace than when we are maturing as His disciples and on mission to make disciples.
- "I personally don't see discipleship as one of the five areas. I believe discipleship is the process and the byproduct of the other four areas along with Bible study and prayer. That is a discussion for another chapter."

Questions to Reflect
- Jesus discipled His disciples who in turn discipled their generation. Have we dropped the baton of

discipleship in our generation? Explain your response.
- In your opinion, what was the connection of prayer and preaching to Pentecost? What other characteristics of Pentecost do you see in Acts 2?
- What are the five focuses of the early church described in Acts 2:42-47?

Chapter 6
Two Weapons for Disciple-Making

Scripture to Discuss
- Acts 2:42
- Ephesians 6:10-20
- Matthew 10:34
- Matthew 26:47-55
- Luke 21:24
- Acts 12:2
- Romans 8:35
- Hebrews 4:12
- Matthew 21:13

Truths to Consider
- The Sword of the Spirit that is the Word of God is a powerful offensive weapon in the hands of the believer.
- A committed prayer life is a powerful offensive weapon in our daily spiritual warfare. A serious commitment to pray for and with each other is a great tool for discipleship.
- It is impossible to take your stand and fight off the adversary without a commitment to God's Word and prayer. We will never be able to grow as disciples of Jesus Christ without a proper understanding and

application of His Word. Since communication is the key component in any relationship, our development as disciples will always be directly proportional to our dedication to prayer.

Questions to Reflect
- How is the sword, the Word of God, being utilized in your life as an offensive weapon towards discipleship?
- How is your current prayer life an offensive weapon for disciple-making?
- How do the six words for prayer in Ephesians 6:18-20 help connect you to a life of discipleship?

Chapter 7
A Discipleship Revolution

Scripture to Discuss
- Acts 2:42, 46
- Acts 1:14
- Acts 6:4
- Colossians 4:2
- Acts 8:13

Truths to Consider
- You don't go to worship, program evangelism, plan discipleship, have a fellowship time, and do ministry. Rather, your passion is Jesus, your burden is for the lost, you want to follow Jesus and mature, you know you can't do it alone, and you are overjoyed that you get to serve Jesus.
- Isn't discipleship the end product of the church? What if worship, evangelism, fellowship, and ministry

were all parts of what it means to become a disciple of Jesus Christ? What if the two offensive weapons of Bible study and prayer are what connect all of these parts? Just maybe we need a transformation in our concept of discipleship.

- The reason the early church did such an awesome job at making disciples is because they were devoted to obeying Christ's command to "make disciples."
- These early Christians faced intense persecution. Yet, they did not allow anything to detour them or distract them from completing the task that God had commanded of them.
- Those of us called by His name must have "A Discipleship Revolution."

Questions to Reflect

- What are your thoughts on the "Discipleship Revolution"?
- What is your response to the statement, "Jesus started the church the way He wanted it! Now, He wants it the way He started it!"?
- Does the biblical word "devoted" found in Acts 2:42 describe your commitment to discipleship? How or why not?
- What can you learn from the example of Philip and Simon in Acts 8:13?

Chapter 8
Worship - The Disciple's Passion

Scripture to Discuss
- Acts 2:43, 47
- Matthew 22:36-40
- Isaiah 6:1, 5
- 1 Kings 18:38-39
- Psalm 96:8-9
- Romans 12:1
- Hebrews 13:15-16
- Psalm 145:2
- Deuteronomy 32:3
- Genesis 22:1-5
- Ezekiel 46:1-2, 8-10

Truths to Consider
- Worship is a part of becoming a disciple of Jesus. It is also a byproduct of discipleship.
- Worship allows me to connect my personal relationship with God with a passionate response to His greatness. No one can give God your personal worship except you.
- The first time you read about worship in Scripture, it is tied to obedience and sacrifice. Worship is not just something you do with your lips; it is also something done with your life!
- "How does worship tie into discipleship?" The answer is simple. You will never devote yourself to following Jesus until you, first of all, love Him deeply.
- True worshippers lead to believers becoming disciples.

Questions to Reflect

- What are your thoughts on Rick Ousley's definition of worship: "Worship is our response to God for who He is and what He has done, expressed in the things we say and the way we live."?
- What do you think of this statement concerning worship: "Worship is a rhythm of revelation and response."?
- Biblical worship is an any-moment, every-day privilege for the believer. Considering that statement, how is worship an integral part of you growing as a disciple?
- How does Ezekiel 46 impact your thoughts on worship?

Chapter 9
Evangelism - The Disciple's Purpose

Scripture to Discuss

- Acts 2:47
- Mark 16:15
- Matthew 28:18-20
- Romans 10:14-15
- Mark 9:37
- John 20:21
- Acts 14:21-22
- Luke 6:13
- Mark 6:30

Truths to Consider

- Discipleship begins and ends with evangelism. Evangelism places a person on the road to discipleship. That road to discipleship leads to evangelism in the life of the believer. Discipleship

isn't complete until further evangelism takes place. Evangelism isn't complete until we are disciples. Evangelism is the purpose for every disciple of Jesus Christ.
- You can't even spell the word Gospel without the word "Go."
- "Live Sold Out." "Live Sent."
- God's plan for His church has always been to save, disciple, and send.

Questions to Reflect
- Are you expecting other people to witness and go, or do you see your responsibility to share the message of Christ?
- In what ways are you living sold out for Jesus?
- How are you living sent?
- Ray Comfort wisely said, "A church that is waiting for sinners to visit their building is like the police waiting for criminals to visit their station." What are your thoughts on this statement?

Chapter 10
Discipleship - The Disciple's Path

Scripture to Discuss
- Acts 2:42
- John 8:31-32
- Luke 14:25-35
- Matthew 5:13

Truths to Consider
- These two offensive weapons for the believer are also the two main tools that lead to discipleship. Bible

study and prayer connect to every area of discipleship. The intentional process of discipleship will require a commitment to God's Word and prayer for any daily development towards discipleship to occur.

- Jesus didn't use the power of His miracles to provide Him a platform to preach an easy pathway to becoming His disciple. He wasn't interested in a crowd of false-converts; He was seeking faithful followers. He didn't preach a health-wealth gospel because the pathway to discipleship is full of sacrifice and surrender.

- We need a revival and renewal of our love-relationship with Jesus Christ. For true biblical discipleship to take place, we need to prioritize our relationship with the Lord. Our dedication to Him will determine our level of discipleship.

Questions to Reflect

- Reflect on Allen Parr's following statements and honestly answer the question: "Are you a Disciple or Just a Christian?"
  - A true disciple elevates faith over family.
  - A true disciple models sacrifice or self-centeredness.
  - A true disciple is willing to accept pain rather than always expecting pleasure.
  - A true disciple elevates relationship over religion.
  - A true disciple values commitment over convenience.
  - A true disciple is useful to God rather than useless.

Chapter 11
Fellowship - The Disciple's Partnership

Scripture to Discuss
- Acts 2:42, 44, 46
- Genesis 1:1-3
- John 1:1-5, 14
- Colossians 1:15-17
- Genesis 1:26-27
- John 17:11
- Ephesians 2:17-22
- Ecclesiastes 4:9-12
- John 15:12-17

Truths to Consider
- Authentic fellowship provides the relational basis for life-on-life discipleship.
- The Bible teaches that God exists eternally in community. It is the mystery of the Trinity. He is the God of fellowship because He lives in community.
- God created us in His own image. He created us in the image of community and therefore, we have a longing built in us for fellowship.
- Our God of fellowship has a goal for fellowship. God desires that His children have the same fellowship as the Trinity shares.
- We belong in a family for fellowship. Being a Christian is not just believing, it is belonging. We need each other and we were created for true fellowship.
- Love forges the believers into a fellowship that produces genuine friends. And biblical fellowship develops believers into disciples that produce much fruit!

Questions to Reflect
- What are your thoughts on our God being the "God of Fellowship"?
- In what specific ways are your pursing the "Goal of Fellowship"?

Chapter 12
Ministry - The Disciple's Posture

Scripture to Discuss
- Acts 2:45
- 1 Corinthians 4:1-2
- Deuteronomy 11:13
- Psalm 105:42
- Deuteronomy 34:5
- 2 Samuel 7:8
- Isaiah 52:13-14
- Isaiah 53:5-7
- Matthew 20:28
- Mark 10:45
- Luke 19:10
- John 10:10

Truths to Consider
- Discipleship leads to ministry and serving Jesus builds disciples. You are never more like Jesus than when you are serving.
- The Old Testament servants all pointed to The Suffering Servant – our Savior. And our Savior calls us to live a life of service.

Questions to Reflect

- What are your thoughts on the picture of an "under-rower" as a servant found in 1 Corinthians 4:1-2?
- In what ways are you like the servants of God found in Scripture?
- What does it mean to your relationship with God that your Savior came as the Servant?
- How important is servanthood in discipleship?

Chapter 13
The Daily Development of Discipleship

Scripture to Discuss

- Any Scripture you want to try with the B.I.B.LE. and P.R.A.Y.E.R acrostics.
- Here are a few suggestions to begin small group study: Mark, Philippians, James.

Truths to Consider

- There is a desperate need in the church today to move people from their decision for Christ to becoming disciples of Christ. We need to move from an aisle we walk down to a path we live out.
- You need an intentional strategy for discipleship.
- The movement from followers to friends takes time and consistency. True disciples are sown and grown not instant and inconsistent. Therefore, this daily development will involve a pathway and a process, not a program and a schedule.
- God would never call us to something that He will not also equip us to become! He desires for disciples who make disciples, and He will grant His power to those devoted to His will. Let's move from decisions

to disciples. May we become all that God desires us to be. Let us not stop short or settle for less. God can lead forgiven people to follow Him to fruitful lives.

Questions to Reflect

- What have you learned from this book that will help you in your development as a disciple of Christ?
- What are your action steps to develop as a disciple of Jesus?

Notes

Chapter 3

1. Ziglar, Z. (n.d.). *Quote*. motivationfortheday.wordpress. com. Retrieved September 16, 2021, from https:// motivationfortheday.wordpress.com/2018/04/13/you-cant-hit-a-target-you-cannot-see-and-you-cannot-see-a-target-you-do-not-have-zig-ziglar-2/

Chapter 6

1. Warren, R. (1995). Myths About Growing Churches. In *Purpose Driven Church* (pp. 49–50). essay, Zondervan.

Chapter 8

1. Ousley, Rick. (2003). From Sermon Series *"Let's Worship: Discovering the Greatness of our God."* Used with permission by author, 2021.
2. Papa, M. (2016, April 19). *Revelation and response (1)*. WORSHIP QUOTABLES. Retrieved January 6, 2022, from https://worr.wordpress.com/2016/04/18/revelation-and-response-1-2/

Chapter 9

1. Stetzer, E. (2016, May 25). *Commentary: Evangelism is central to calling of Christianity*. https://www. inquirer.com. Retrieved November 10, 2021, from https://www.inquirer.com/philly/opinion/20160525_ Commentary__Evangelism_is_central_to_calling_ of_Christianity.html

2. Greear, J. D. (2016, March 16). *20 quotes from "gaining by losing"*. 20 Quotes from "Gaining by Losing" – JD Greear Ministries. Retrieved October 4, 2021, from https://jdgreear.com/20-quotes-from-gaining-by-losing/

3. Ministries, L. F., Ministries, L. F., & says:, R. C. (2018, March 17). *7 concerns and challenges*. Connecting with You! Retrieved December 5, 2021, from https://connectingwithyou.net/2018/02/28/7-concerns-and-challenges/#: ~:text=As%20evangelist%20Ray%20Comfort%20has%20written%3A%20'%20A,to%20every%20Christian%20to%20play%20our%20part%20and

4. Greear, J. D. (2015, July 8). *The church isn't a cruise ship; it's an aircraft carrier*. The Church Isn't a Cruise Ship; It's an Aircraft Carrier – JD Greear Ministries. Retrieved November 20, 2021, from https://jdgreear.com/the-church-isnt-a-cruise-ship-its-an-aircraft-carrier/#:~:text=Study%20after%20study%20shows%20that%20most%20Christians%20have,we%20get%20away%20with%20using%20the%20name%20"evangelical"%21%29

5. Edington, S., & Cranston, D. (2021, June 14). *The power of praying women*. Just Between Us Magazine. Retrieved January 2, 2022, from https://justbetweenus.

org/everyday-faith/power-of-prayer/the-power-of-praying-women/

Chapter 10

1. Parr, A. (2017, November 7). *Are you a disciple or just a Christian? | 10-minute sermons.* YouTube. Retrieved December 10, 2021, from https://www.youtube.com/watch?v=acdctMh2HWM.

About The Author

Dr. Ray Cummings has pastored churches in Mississippi and Alabama and has served in ministry for over 30 years. He now resides in Purvis, Mississippi and serves Hattiesburg Community Church as an Associate Pastor. He is a graduate of William Carey College and New Orleans Baptist Theological Seminary. He and his wife, Amanda have been blessed with 4 children and one daughter-in-law: Carter and Hope, Camron, Moses, and Mercy. They have a non-profit named after their daughter called "Mercy's Mission" that feeds and educates children in an orphanage in Goma, Congo.

Ray is the co-author for the 41series.com. He loves preaching, writing, hunting, and anything sports related.

Made in the USA
Columbia, SC
02 March 2025

54597930R00072